Miracles Can Happen!

MODERN STORIES OF HOPE AND HEALING

LESLEY SUSSMAN

Printed in the United States of America
Halo Press is a trademark of Ottenheimer Publishers, Inc.
10 Church Lane, Baltimore, Maryland 21208, USA
RE-499B

To my father, Max, who has long worked miracles in other people's lives by cheering them up with a smile and a song.

Contents

Foreword

I did not arrive at my fundamental understanding of the laws of the Universe through my rational mind.

ALBERT EINSTEIN

As a psychologist and researcher, I have investigated medical miracles for many years. In medical journals, I refer to these cases as "significant aberrations from medically established norms." Most journals would not publish works that referred to "miracles"—it would be considered unscientific. In truth, however, "miracle" seems more accurate, for neither science nor our rational minds can explain what has happened to these people.

Miracles of all kinds happen every day. Yet, because most of us have been taught that reasonable human beings do not believe in miracles, we are blind to them when they occur. In many ways, Walter Purlington's story is typical of "extraordinary survivors."

When Walter was diagnosed with carcinomatosis (cancer of the spinal fluid), his doctor felt that there was less than one chance in one thousand that he could survive even one year. Two local oncologists confirmed that he had contracted this lethal disease. He was so ill that all treatment, except for basic care needed to ease his discomfort, was discontinued. He was referred to a hospice, where they anticipated his imminent death.

Walter has done more than just survive in the 12 years that have passed since this diagnosis—he has thrived. This 60-year-old man chops his own firewood, rides his snowmobile every chance he gets, and makes fishing excursions to Alaska. He is cancer free.

When I asked Walter's oncologist why he thought Walter had such an extraordinary course of illness, the doctor told me that he now assumes the original diagnosis must have been a mistake.

I was incredulous. Walter's diagnosis had been independently established by three local physicians. International experts on carcinomatosis at Duke University confirmed beyond doubt the accuracy of the diagnosis. I asked Walter's oncologist why he now believes a mistake had been made. He indicated that the answer seemed rather obvious: "Everyone knows that no one survives the type of cancer that he was supposed to have."

Spontaneous regression is probably the closest term that medicine has for a miracle. (Regression is considered spontaneous when a malignant tumor disappears or shrinks significantly, and medical treatment cannot adequately account for the improved condition.) The medical literature maintains that spontaneous regression is phenomenally rare—occurring only once in every 60,000 to 100,000 cases. But cases such as Walter's are never counted. Hundreds, perhaps thousands, of others are also excluded.

The gift of Les Sussman's book is apparent even in the title: he lets us know that, indeed, *miracles do happen!* The rich array of stories also suggests that miracles are more common than usually believed, though no less magnificent. In an age in which we tend to relegate the wisdom of the heart far beneath the head, true stories such as these can help restore our equilibrium. Our spirits are lifted because they provide a way for us to glimpse the absolute wonder of the universe.

PAUL ROUD, PH.D., M.ED.
Author of *Making Miracles*

Preface

Nowadays, whenever someone finds out that I've written this book, I'm asked the same question over and over again: What is a miracle?

And each time, I patiently try to explain that a miracle is not something that lends itself to a precise definition. It's like asking, "What does God look like?" Everyone imagines the Divine differently.

Is it a miracle when someone diagnosed with terminal cancer is given a few months to live and is still alive and well 12 years later, with the disease in complete remission? I think so, although there are others who might describe it as "luck," a "fluke," "mind over matter," or something else having nothing at all to do with divine intervention.

Choose your own interpretation. After writing this book, I've become convinced that there are more things in heaven and earth than twentieth-century science would have us believe. There are occurrences that transcend the natural order of events. And until someone can prove—not just speculate—otherwise, "miracle" seems an appropriate word for me.

Finally, I just want to thank all the people whose true stories appear in this book for their willingness to share them. I fervently hope that this book—as it has for me—inspires everyone who reads it to search for the miraculous in their own lives. . . .

Acknowledgments

Like an Academy Award nominee, I'm trying to keep short the list of people whom I'd like to thank for helping make this book possible. Wish I had a couple of pages to name them all.

Special thanks to Claire Gerus, who conceived the idea for the book, and Tori Banks, my editor, who makes writers look good in the final product.

Also thanks to Alan Grossman and Andrea Shaw for meals and moral support during the writing of the book, and other friends as well—like Sally, Patricia and Karyn. Many thanks for leads on miracle stories to freelance writer Alan Ebert, Jim Blue of the Veterans Administration Regional Office in New York City, Beverly Williston of the *National Star*, and psychologist Paul Roud. Many thanks as well to Toronto radio talk show host Alan Mayer, and, especially, to Joanne D.S. McMahon, Director of the Parapsychology Foundation Library in New York City. And let me not forget Morris Sobel, my uncle, who convinced a Holocaust survivor to tell her remarkable story. Lastly, thanks to Grace Furst of the California Society for Psychical Study for the free ad.

A Rocky Mountain Miracle

Over the years, there have been many stories of humans being rescued by a variety of animals—from dolphins to dogs.

But when 16-year-old Ryan Potton got lost for more than 12 hours in a Rocky Mountain blizzard, some animals not ordinarily known for making contact with humans may very well have saved his life.

Wearing only light clothing and suffering from hypothermia, the Denver teenager woke up in the middle of the night to find that nature had provided a very special blanket. Huddling next to Ryan were two female elk who kept him warm until rescuers found him the following morning....

Ryan Potton is a tall, husky 18-year-old who works in light construction in Denver, Colorado. He says he will never forget that September day in 1992 when he became separated from his father and friends while grouse hunting high in the Rockies.

"It was September 4th, and we'd gone for a three-day hunting weekend," he recalls. "The weather was pretty good, and all I was wearing were jeans, a T-shirt, a light jacket and a hunting vest."

When Ryan spotted grouse up on a ridge, he decided to go after them. He didn't think much about heading out on his own. Most of the group had hunted in these mountains before and the teenager thought he knew the area well.

He was mistaken. "I was retracing my steps down the ridge to where my dad was, but I must have missed the road," he recalls. "The trail markers on the trees were very confusing." Ryan lost his way back. Eventually, he followed a trail that took him in a circle. He found himself back where he had started.

By then, a sudden freezing rainstorm was hitting the area. Ryan's father and friends decided to return to their campsite. No one really worried about the boy. They expected him to turn up later, as he had done on other hunting trips. By evening, however, Ryan's father realized that something was wrong. He called the Sheriff's Department to report his son missing.

Ryan remembers how terror began to set in. "I was scared. I was screaming and yelling and shooting off rounds, but no one heard me." Still hoping to find the right trail, the 16-year-old kept walking until he was exhausted. The temperature had now dropped to freezing, and Ryan tried to start a fire with black powder from his rifle shells. The mixture of snow and rain kept it from working.

"I was exhausted, so I lay down under some trees to rest. I tried to keep my wits about me. I figured if I stayed in one place a rescue team would find me." Temperatures continued to plummet as Ryan settled for the night. Heavy snow began to fall. Lost in the dark and shivering uncontrollably—one of the first stages of hypothermia—Ryan began to slip into sleep. From that moment on, things are a bit unclear to him, even to this day.

Ryan recalls being awakened by the sounds of animals moving about in the darkness. "I threw stones at them. I thought they might be coyotes and I tried to scare them off." A few minutes later the animals returned. Although still frightened, Ryan says he tried to overcome his fear and get a better look at what was out there. He lifted his rifle and moments later put it back down, relieved. They weren't coyotes, after all, but a small herd of elk.

What happened next still amazes Ryan. Although he cradled his shotgun on his lap, the elk fearlessly approached him. "They came very close to me. I wasn't scared anymore, just curious. I had never seen elk that close before."

Exhausted, Ryan drifted off to sleep, awakening briefly some hours later. This time, however, he awoke feeling "warm and comfortable." Looking around, he quickly understood why. "Two of the elk were there—lying next to me. I don't know how else I would have stayed warm through the night."

When Ryan awoke the next morning, the elk were gone. He took off again, drinking from a waterfall and trying to ignore the cold. "I kept thinking that no one was going to ever find me. I didn't even know they had a search party out for me at the time."

He was wrong. In fact, a search party had been looking for him all night long.

At about 4:30 A.M., the rescue team got its first break. Hasty, one of the search dogs, began to pick up Ryan's scent. The team followed Hasty and made slow progress as it struggled through marshes.

"The majority of the time we were in the clouds and the visibility was approximately 50 feet," Dan Burnett, leader of one of the search teams, recalls. "We were using our compasses to keep from getting lost ourselves."

Then came the unbelievable news. At 9:30 A.M., word came over portable radios that Ryan had been found alive.

He was wet and cold, but he didn't show any signs of frostbite. How was this possible? After all, it was the kind of weather that would ordinarily kill anyone without shelter within two hours.

When Dan and the other rescuers listened to Ryan's story, they could hardly believe it. Elk are elusive creatures not known to approach humans. The rescuers decided to check out Ryan's story. What they found was startling. "We found depressions in the snow where the elk had been," Dan states. "There was absolutely no other explanation for his survival that I could come up with."

He is not alone in thinking so. Lt. Derrick Woodman of the Summit Sheriff's Department, also a member of the search team, adds: "Wearing the kind of clothes he was, there was some reason why he walked away from that alive." Woodman's superior, Summit County Sheriff Delbert Ewoldt, echoes that sentiment. "Something special must have happened up there for Ryan to have survived."

As for Ryan, he's back grouse hunting in those very same mountains. The one thing he says he will never hunt is—you guessed it—elk.

Baby Saved by Mother's Plea for Prayers

Should you someday soon visit Erie, Pennsylvania, and happen to pass by the local athletic field, you might spot a group of youngsters having a great time playing soccer or another favorite sport.

There is a strong likelihood that eight-year-old Eric Danowski, with his sandy brown hair and big dark eyes, will be among them, and you just might want to say hello to this very special boy.

That's because when he was only 10 months old, he was given little hope for survival by his doctors. But Eric, the victim of a rare liver disorder that twice brought him to the brink of death, is still here today, as healthy as a kid can be, and all because of what his mother describes as the miracle of prayer....

It was the kind of news that no mother ever wants to hear. On a cold February day in 1988, Debbie Danowski, an administrative assistant for a local insurance company, learned that her two-month-old son, Eric, had a rare and life-threatening disorder affecting his liver.

Eight heart-breaking months later, Eric's condition had

deteriorated so badly that the child was rushed to Pittsburgh's Children's Hospital, where on October 21 he underwent his first liver transplant.

"Eric was in a coma and was very, very frail. The doctors didn't even know if he would make it through the transplant, but he did."

But that was only the beginning of Eric's ordeal, for the liver transplant was unsuccessful. Eric would require a second operation in order to survive.

The news brought his usually positive, outgoing mother to tears. "I felt that something was very wrong, and that he would continue to get worse even with another liver transplant. The nurses kept telling me that I was wrong, but I had this gut feeling."

Her instincts would prove to be correct.

On March 3—after a statewide appeal by television stations and the mayor of Erie—another liver was donated and Eric underwent his second transplant. This time the surgery was successful, and Eric's doctors were pleased by the results.

But as Debbie had feared, it was a short-lived triumph. Serious complications soon set in. Severe pneumonia struck Eric, coating the child's lungs with a gluey mucous, slowly smothering him. Doctors told Debbie that 90 percent of transplant patients who contracted such a virus failed to survive. And Eric was initially in a weakened condition.

Debbie's voice is tinged with sadness as she recalls those dreadful days. "He was so frail; the doctors put him in a sand bed because bones were breaking through his back. At one point, the doctors told us he wasn't going to make it."

However, Eric did make it. Although the boy was hooked up to a ventilator in the Intensive Care Unit, doctors made an exception on April 2 and allowed him to have visitors. After all, it was his first birthday!

"The doctors allowed 19 members of my family to come in and sing 'Happy Birthday' to him," Debbie recalls with laughter. "It was a special moment for my entire family."

Six days later, Eric was released from intensive care. A headline in the local paper proclaimed: "Easter Miracle Baby Winning Fight For Life." But Eric was far from being out of danger. Many of his serious symptoms persisted, and didn't seem to show any signs of improving. Eric needed another transplant, but the doctors didn't think he was strong enough to survive the operation.

It was then that Debbie decided to seek a kind of help that sidestepped traditional medicine. She visited the

Erie Daily Times, and pleaded with the editors to print a story asking people to pray for her baby boy.

Reporter Jack Grazier responded to the young woman's plea. His article appeared in the paper's evening edition. The story began, "Debbie Danowski is asking for your prayers to help her baby live." The story ended with a reminder that Debbie was hoping readers could do for her child what medicine apparently could not: create a healing miracle.

"The article ran on Friday," Debbie says. "That night I went to bed and I told God I was tired of fighting with Him. I wanted Eric to get better, but things really weren't getting much better."

When Debbie arrived at the hospital the following morning, she received some extraordinary news. Doctors excitedly told her that Eric's lungs were clearing, his fever had disappeared, and the child's vital signs had greatly improved. One doctor turned to her and said: "As of now, I would say that Eric has beaten the virus."

She remembers the stir that the news of Eric's sudden improvement created at the hospital. "Some of the doctors really couldn't believe that Eric had made such a swift recovery," she says.

Eric was pronounced healthy enough to undergo a third liver transplant. This time, however, not only was the transplant a success, but there were no complications. Just 17 days later, the "miracle baby" was out of the hospital and on his way home.

Debbie concludes: "Here's a child who had three liver transplants within 10 months. He was close to death, in a coma, with two days to live at one point. I think it was the prayer groups who continued to pray for Eric that made his total recovery take place."

Jack Grazier, the reporter who wrote the story on baby Eric, agrees. "Was it a miracle caused by the power of prayer? I can't say. But I know that this child was dying—that doctors were doing a deathwatch—when people all over this town started praying. Should I ever be in such a life-threatening situation, I hope people put their prayers together for me."

Miracles from a Plane Crash

"Anyone who has survived a plane crash knows what miracles are all about," says Jerry Schemmel, the radio play-by-play announcer of the Denver Nuggets basketball team.

And as a survivor of one of the worst airline crashes in the United States, Jerry says he has experienced several miracles firsthand.

Not only did the veteran sportscaster survive the crash in which 112 people were killed, but he even managed to pull off something of a miracle himself. Jerry crawled back into the wreckage from which he had just emerged to rescue a baby girl whose parents believed their daughter was dead. . . .

"So many miracles happened on that plane—it's impossible not to believe in miracles," Jerry Schemmel says. He wastes little time in rattling off just a few of the miracles that he witnessed before and after the crash.

Like the child who was rescued from the wreckage:

"The little girl that I picked up was in row 27 or 28," he recalls. "She had been sitting on the floor between her mother's feet in row 11. She had been thrown almost 20 rows, but the extent of her injuries was a cut under her eye. To me, that's an absolute miracle."

And the number of people who survived the impact:

"If you saw the videotape of the crash and the fireball and all the devastation, it's miraculous that there were 184 survivors."

As well as the exceptional navigational skill of the pilot in keeping the plane aloft until it reached an airport:

"Even to get to Sioux City—the fact that we had a chance to land at an airport—that was a miracle in itself. I talked to Captain Al Haynes, who was in the cockpit that day, and he said 'I still don't know how we made it to Sioux City. We took off, started to make right turns and all of a sudden we were there.'"

Several years afterward, speaking from his Houston hotel room, Jerry recalls that fateful summer day on July 19, 1989, a day that he was certain he was going to die.

Jerry was then deputy commissioner and legal counsel of the Continental Basketball Association. He was flying from Denver to Chicago with one of his best friends, Jay Ramsdell, CBA commissioner at the time. Ironically, the two men had boarded United Airlines flight 232 in Denver after an earlier flight had been canceled because of mechanical difficulties.

"We were the last two passengers to board," he says. "They gave us seats in different sections of the plane. About an hour into the flight an explosion in one of the engines crippled the craft's hydraulic system."

The airliner was only about 15 minutes from the Sioux City airport at the time of the explosion but because the damage was so severe, the pilot later told reporters he was not certain he could keep the aircraft aloft until it could reach the airport.

But he managed to do exactly that, skillfully keeping the plane in the air by balancing the remaining engines. Once over the airport, the pilot took the aircraft down, crash-landing with a terrifying jolt.

Jerry remembers the sickening sound of crunching metal as the plane started to flip over, and how passengers were violently rocked in their seats. He recalls the bumping noises and the screech of metal as the bottom of the plane dragged along the runway and broke up into sections.

"Rows 22 to about 30—the section I ended up in—flipped over once and slid along the runway upside down. Then it slid off the right side of the runway into a cornfield."

Jerry, hanging upside down and still strapped to his seat, viewed the horror all around him from his awkward position. "The guy next to me was dead," he says. "The woman across from me was gone. The flight attendant who'd been in the jump seat facing me was gone." So was his friend, Jay—one of the 112 victims of the crash.

The sportscaster says he unbuckled his safety belt and tumbled down to the floor, which was the ceiling of the upside-down aircraft. "There was no way out," he says. "I didn't see sunlight or an opening, no exit whatsoever."

The compartment was rapidly filling up with smoke. Jerry remembers thinking: "I've survived, but now I'm going to burn up or suffocate because I can't get out."

Jerry eventually spotted sunlight pouring through an opening in the twisted metal where the front section of the plane had been, and knew that escape was possible. Despite an injured back, a sprained ankle, smoke inhalation, and abrasions, he and several other passengers—including two-time U.S. Olympic equestrian Michael Matz—pulled dazed passengers to their feet and pushed them out of the plane.

"I tried to help a couple of people, and there were other men who, like me, were hurt seriously but were helping people to their feet."

Instead of escaping immediately, Jerry continued to assist passengers until the smoke grew so thick he was forced to leave the plane. "I couldn't see, let alone breathe at that point," he recalls.

Once outside the plane, Jerry says his first reaction was to run as far as possible from the twisted wreckage, in case it exploded. "In the movies and on TV every time you get outside of something, it explodes. That was what I was thinking about."

But then Jerry heard a baby crying inside the wreckage. He changed his mind and crawled back into the plane on all fours, following the sound of the child's sobs. Toward the middle of the plane he found the infant girl partially buried in debris.

"I wasn't trying to be a hero. It was just something that happened. It was an instinctive thing. I didn't even think about it."

When Jerry emerged from the cornfield carrying the infant in his arms, the baby's parents could not believe it. They were sure their baby was dead.

"It was a miracle that my baby was still alive," says Lori Michaelson, the child's mother. "I didn't think she even had a chance."

Jerry says that in the 44 minutes from the time the engine blew until the plane crashed, he did a lot of praying. "I thought for a long time that I was gone, that my number was up. I was completely convinced of that. We all knew it was a very, very dangerous situation."

Since the accident, the sportscaster says he has become a devout Christian. "I think my priorities have been reorganized for the better," Jerry says. "I put my religious convictions first, and everything else falls behind that—even whether the Nuggets win or lose a game," he quips.

A Military Man's Dream Comes True

For as long as he could remember, Mike Scotto dreamed about becoming a military officer. When marital problems eventually wreaked havoc on his Army career and forced him to leave the service, Mike's dream suddenly turned into a nightmare.

But a chance visit to a small Columbus, Georgia, bookstore proved to be the miracle that turned his life around. Today, Mike is back in the service as a Lieutenant Colonel in the U.S. Army Reserves—where he is again pursuing a dream he thought had vanished forever. . . .

It was 1974, and 22-year-old Smithtown, New York, resident Mike Scotto was leading what appeared to be a picture-perfect life. The ROTC scholarship winner had recently graduated with honors, married his pretty high school sweetheart, and had begun raising a family.

Mike's ambition to become an army officer was also off to a quick start. Almost immediately after graduating, he was called up for active duty in Fort Benning, Georgia, where Mike planned to pursue a 30-year military career.

But from the moment he arrived in Georgia, Mike says he felt as if the bottom had fallen out of his life.

"I had a lot of problems with my wife," he says. "She began running up bills and doing other things that drastically and negatively affected my career."

He notes that in the military "a good wife doesn't make your career. But if you're having problems—especially financial ones—they sure can destroy it." Unfortunately, Mike was having those kinds of problems.

Mike says word of his problems at home reached his superiors. His next efficiency report recommended that he be dismissed from the service when he completed his term.

The career soldier was crushed. "I had spent two years with a very difficult outfit. It was a training brigade, and believe it or not that was the only place I was happy," he says. "I worked with a couple of very wonderful people there who both became four-star generals, and I learned a lot from them."

It was Mike's dream to earn those stars, too. But all his hard work had amounted to nothing. Instead of a promotion, Mike was repeatedly passed over for his captain's stripes. Mike's superiors were sending him a clear message about his future in the military.

Discouraged and unable to resolve the situation with his wife, Mike decided to resign from the Army. At the same time, his problems at home worsened. Mike's wife left him, and he suddenly found himself a single father with three young children to raise.

One afternoon, Mike was in Columbus, Georgia, and went into a small bookstore. *Power and Praise*, a book written by Merlin Curruthers, a former paratrooper, caught Mike's attention.

"I picked it up for two reasons," he says. "First of all, it talked about power. I said, 'Yes, that's what I need.' The other thing I happened to notice was that the author was a former military man."

He quickly discovered that the "power" discussed in the book was a spiritual one. "The power was in accepting not what God has done, but rather what God has let happen in order to draw you closer to Him," he says. "When you get beaten up enough, you go down on your knees. And that's kind of what had happened to me."

Mike could not put the book down, amazed at how closely it related to his life. "When I finished reading it, I looked up and said: 'Okay, Jesus, I've made a mess out of my life. You do what you want.'"

When Mike awoke the next morning, none of his problems had disappeared, but something had definitely changed. "I just felt as if I had been incredibly, monumentally transformed," he says.

Now 27 years old, Mike left Georgia and returned to his family in New York state. It was there that he began to notice a new, more positive force guiding his efforts.

Mike responded to an advertisement in the paper for a job selling coins and stamps, "which I knew absolutely nothing about." He was turned down, but five minutes later the phone rang. The employer, a former Air Force officer, had reconsidered. He offered Mike the job.

"First, I got a job almost five minutes after the interviewer turned me down. Then, I was paid twice as much as everyone was telling me I could expect to be paid. That's an incredible miracle when you have three kids to feed."

Mike says other positive experiences followed. Yet something continued to bother him. "I still had one nagging failure, and it was like a bug in my soup," he says. "I really wanted a career in the Army."

Which is when a second miracle took place in his life.

"One day I got a letter from the Army's Reserve Personnel Center," he recalls. "It essentially said that I should call them about my career. I said to myself, 'What career?'" But he called anyway, remembering that he felt "ashamed and embarrassed about my lousy record." Mike told "the whole sorry story" to his personnel manager.

When he finished speaking, the manager said to him: "Listen, the review board just met to decide on captain promotions. Let me put you on hold and see if you made it." Mike thought the man was joking. Although he knew his name had automatically been placed on the U.S. Army Reserve's promotion list despite leaving the military, what chance did he have with his record?

The manager was off the phone before Mike could tell him not to bother. While he waited for the personnel manager to return, he fumed. "I gave God a piece of my mind," he chuckles. "I said, 'Listen, God, I've been pretty good lately and I don't deserve to be humiliated like this.'"

A few minutes later, Mike received news that caused his jaw to drop. "The personnel manager said, 'Well, congratulations. You made it. You're a captain.'" Mike was back in the military.

Today, at 42, Mike holds the rank of Lieutenant Colonel in the U.S. Army Reserves. Thinking back, he views what happened to him that day as another miracle. "The good

Lord, Himself, gave me that one," he says. "He was more than generous.

"It all started with this book that happened to catch my eye. That book helped me mend my ways and look toward a different path."

Six Minutes in Another Dimension

For six long minutes, as doctors in a Michigan hospital desperately struggled to start her heart beating again, Carol Woodard says her spirit soared to a place of light and beauty far removed from the operating table—a place she did not wish to leave and still thinks about with a sense of longing.

When Carol reluctantly returned from that "paradise," it was not empty-handed. She says she brought back with her a very special gift—the gift of healing. . . .

On April 3, 1970, Carol Woodard was being prepared for the Caesarean-section birth of her fourth child at Cottage Hospital in Grosse Point, Michigan.

Although the young woman had given birth three times before in the same manner, she recalls that this time things felt darkly wrong. But no one paid much attention to her concerns. She grimaces at the memory.

"I'm usually an easygoing person with a very mild personality, but I kept telling my doctors, my husband, the anesthesiologist and any nurse who would listen to me that something wasn't right. I just knew it wasn't right. I knew that something was going to go wrong with the surgery," the petite graphic artist recalls.

Instead, they told Carol, who today works for a newspaper in Martinez, Georgia, that she was suffering a severe case of nerves.

"They tried to calm me down," Carol, now 52, recalls, "telling me that I was young and had successfully delivered my other children through C-sections." Still, she continued to resist. "I kept saying, 'No, something is not right.' I told them I didn't want to have the surgery. I begged them not to do it, or at least to postpone it."

Carol's high state of anxiety prompted a visit by the hospital's anesthesiologist. He told her that if she wanted to have a healthy baby, the surgery could not be delayed. She reluctantly agreed.

"They prepped me, gave me a sedative to relax me, and took me into the surgery room," Carol recalls. "They were still cleaning up from the previous surgery, so I lay on a gurney over on the side of the room."

What Carol saw in those moments petrified her so, she remembers it clearly, even today. "The room took on an eerie glow. I can still visualize it. I can still see it so clearly,

24 years later." There is a long pause as she plays that image through her mind.

She also remembers thinking that the eerie-looking room would be the last sight that she would ever see. "By then, the relaxant they had given me had kicked in. I didn't have any strength to fight against having the surgery."

Carol was placed on the surgical table. Moments later, the anesthesiologist she had spoken to earlier that day entered the room. "He reassured me that he was going to be very careful not to hurt me, and he gave me my spinal."

The last thing Carol recalls seeing is the anesthesiologist's eyes watching her. "I started to say, 'I... can't... br....' I don't even think I got the word 'breathe' out, and I stopped breathing."

The surgery began at 9 A.M. By 9:17 A.M., doctors had delivered a healthy baby girl. Somewhere in that time frame, however, Carol Woodard's heart stopped beating. She lost six minutes of her life and entered a completely different dimension of time and space.

"I was out of my body. I saw the surgery room and the doctors below me. I vaguely remember gazing down at the whole scene and thinking, 'Oh, I don't want to be bothered with it.'"

What she did find fascinating was "this beautiful blue-white light. I wanted to close my eyes, because I just knew its intensity would be painful. I couldn't look at it, it was so bright."

The light had no focal point, but she was nonetheless attracted to it. "I just wanted to go to it. I knew there was something else going on (in the surgery room), but I just didn't care."

The closer Carol moved toward the light, the more it filled her with an indescribable feeling of love. Her voice grows soft as she draws from the well of memory. "It was like looking at the Grand Canyon. I remember once sitting there looking at it in awe, wordlessly. There just weren't words for this feeling, either. It was all-encompassing. It engulfed me."

The light also filled her with feelings of peace and tranquility. Then she had a startling revelation. "I sensed that there were other—I want to call them beings—but at the time I thought of them as other lights. But they weren't as bright as this one. This one was just as bright as can be."

Carol remembers believing at the time that the brightest light was Jesus Christ. "I felt the others were there, but I didn't know who or what they were," she says.

She continued to bask in the primary bright light, feeling "extremely loving and peaceful." But soon a gentle male voice interrupted her astral reverie.

"I was being told that I couldn't stay—that I had things to do. The voice told me I had to go back. And I remember being pulled back through a tunnel, and it emotionally hurt me. I didn't want to go back."

There is a sense of wonder in Carol's voice as she describes her return to her physical body. "I was moving backward very quickly, and as I glanced to the side of me there were windows with different time periods in the history of Earth."

Carol recalls seeing images outside those windows of people dressed as they did in the sixteenth century and earlier. "They were impressions I had. I was moving backward so quickly I didn't have time to study the figures."

The next thing that Carol remembers is being back on the surgical table and looking up at her doctors who were pounding on her chest. She laughs at the memory. "They seemed to be working very hard," she says. "I remember nurses yelling my name, slapping my face, arms and legs."

For the next two days, the hospital's medical staff kept a close watch on Carol. She recalls with amusement how tight-lipped the medical staff was about what had happened during those extraordinary moments when she had lost consciousness.

"They didn't want to admit that something had gone wrong. When I asked my doctor, all he would say was that the delivery was very difficult."

It was from that time on that Carol says her life dramatically changed. "Since then I've had dreams and visions—psychic experiences that I couldn't explain."

For example, Carol recalls that when she returned home from the hospital with her new baby, "it was like I had never been there before. It took me a week or so to get acclimated to my own home and my children. I just felt I didn't belong there."

Other strange incidents also plagued her and continue to do so even today. She would know, and often still knows in advance, that her telephone was going to ring and who would be calling. Carol also experienced several precognitive dreams about future events.

One of the most important differences in Carol's life was a newfound ability to heal people. Carol discovered that she had this ability in 1982, while she was taking classes at a local college. Carol was working after school in a photography laboratory, when another woman in the laboratory became suddenly ill. "She had trouble breathing and was starting to turn gray," Carol recalls.

Carol started to call for an ambulance, but at that moment she heard a voice saying, "Place your hands on her neck." She did so, and the result was incredible. She could feel energy pouring from her hands into the woman's body.

Within 20 minutes the woman was breathing normally once again.

"I'm a healing-touch practitioner now. I put my hands on people who are ill. When I work on people it's as if I see more than their body. I can feel all the energy around them, and I can feel the different layers. I can even sense what's going on in each layer."

In fact, her healing skills are so strong that when Carol recently healed a man who had been injured in an automobile accident, she could "not only see his injury—and this may seem strange—but I could see the pain the body was in, as well."

Carol admits that her ability to heal puzzled her at first. "I wanted to know why I had these powers, what was going on? Why me? I studied anything I could find to try to get an answer."

Still perplexed three years later, Carol finally decided to pay a visit to Dr. George Rogers, the physician who was at her side during the operation when she had her out-of-body experience.

Carol remembers that the doctor was an elderly man close to retirement at the time of her visit. "I sat down with him and said, 'Dr. Rogers, you've just got to talk to me.'"

"I told him everything that had happened to me since that day. I told him I wasn't going to sue him. I just wanted to know what happened to me that day in surgery."

She recollects that Dr. Rogers was not quick to answer her question. Then she learned for the first time the events of that morning on the surgical table.

"He looked at me and said, 'What do you think happened?'

"I said, 'Did I die? Did something else more than just the surgery happen?'"

Finally, she received the answer she had been seeking for years.

"He said, 'Yes, you did. Your heart stopped beating for six minutes, and we had quite a time getting you back.' He told me this conversation was off the record and that he would not admit to it even if I took him to court."

Carol's out-of-body experience was only the beginning of her search for spiritual meaning. "It changed my whole life. I know now that I'm more than just a physical being. We're all much more than that, and we each have to start our own search for the miraculous...."

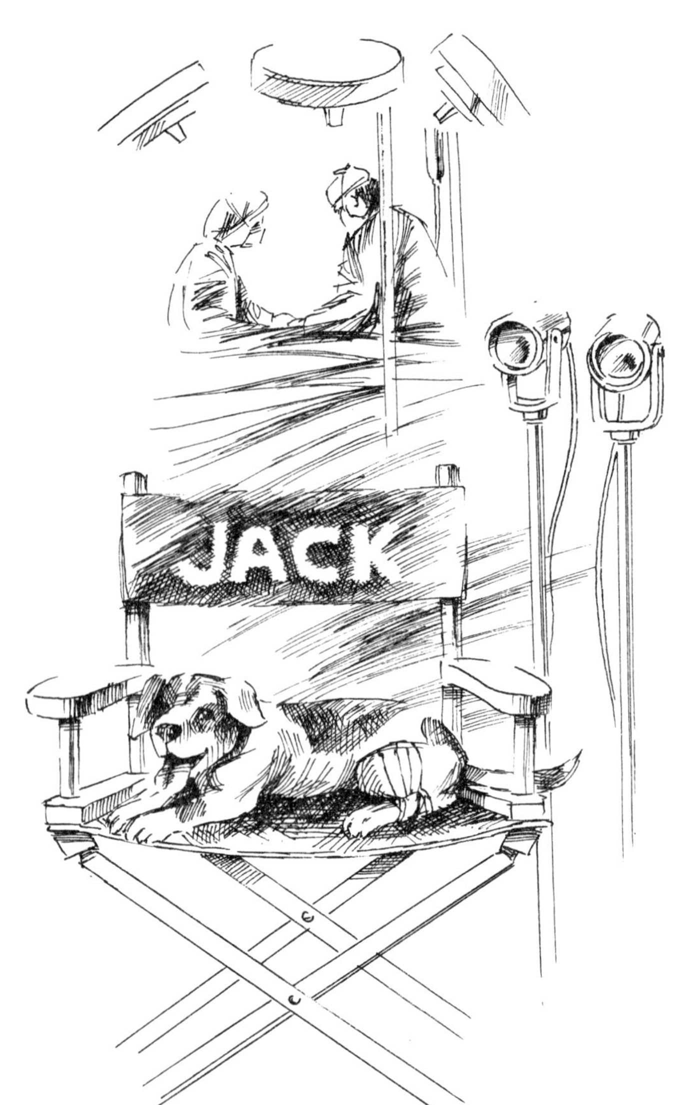
JACK

From Street Mutt to Top Dog: Jack's Story

For Jack, the miracle mutt, December 31, 1993 was nothing to scratch a flea at. Homeless and hungry, Jack, a one-year-old mixed breed, forlornly wandered the streets of Manhattan. He was too busy scavenging for food to do any New Year's Eve revelling.

When he was struck by a bus that evening and nearly fatally injured, little did he know that the accident would prove to be a blessing in disguise. It would become the start of developments that would transform a miserable mutt into a miracle one, and put an end to his bad-luck life....

"Jack is one dog that no one at New York City's American Society for the Prevention of Cruelty to Animals will ever forget," says Bobbi Keene, the agency's public relations coordinator.

And it's likely that Jack will never forget the people at the ASPCA who went out of their way to save his life.

"Jack was hurt on New Year's Eve," recalls Bobbi. "A woman saw it happen, picked him up, and brought him to a veterinary hospital in Greenwich Village."

Jack's back leg was completely crushed in the accident, and the dog was in shock. Doctors at the veterinary hospital told Jack's rescuer that it would cost nearly $4,000 to save the dog's life. The woman simply could not afford such expensive care.

Fortunately for Jack, his rescuer recalled seeing an evening news program in which Gene Mederos, the ASPCA's Director of Adoption, had appeared. "Gene would go on every week with an animal we were trying to adopt," Bobbi says.

"The woman contacted Gene and told him the story. Gene told her, 'Bring the dog over and we'll take care of him.' There were enough funds left that we could afford to treat him."

Bobbi and the staff immediately fell in love with the hapless canine. "He was the sweetest, kindest dog we've ever seen here. We originally named him 'Bagel' because he was hit in front of a bagel store."

Bagel, or Jack as he is called today, remained in the ASPCA's intensive care unit for almost four months. "He had his own little pad in that unit. The staff members made up a little name tag for him and decorated his pad with all kinds of flowers and colors."

Jack continued to undergo treatment for his severe injuries. "He had a series of skin grafts and his hind legs were reconstructed by our orthopedic surgeon," Bobbi says. "We put him all back together again."

Four months later, Jack experienced another miracle in his life. Someone wanted to adopt him. Steve Walker, a producer from the FX cable network, arrived at the animal shelter seeking a "gentle and trainable one-year-old mixed-breed dog." Walker told her the cable network planned to feature the dog on a nationally syndicated pet show.

"Immediately, both Gene and I thought of Bagel," Bobbi says. "We walked Steve through the shelter, brought out a couple of dogs and were sitting and talking when Gene went upstairs to bring Bagel down."

It was love at first bark between the television producer and the miracle dog. "Steve heard his story and said that this was the dog they were looking for."

Approximately two weeks later, the producer returned with his film crew and adopted Bagel. "Today this dog is all better," Bobbi says. "His leg is great, he runs, and Steve works with him to therapeutically exercise his leg."

Bagel, who was renamed Jack for show-business reasons, has become something of a television celebrity.

The miracle dog is seen on television as the co-host of "The Pet Department," a nationally syndicated cable program on the FX network.

In his spare time, Jack does volunteer work for the ASPCA. "He came back and served as our mascot for the dog walk we sponsored the other month," Bobbi says. "He's also done some other volunteer work for us."

Jack is certainly a miracle dog, Bobbi admits. "This dog went through a heck of a lot. We think of him as the doggy version of the rags to riches story. He went from life on the streets and being hit by a bus, to being driven around town in a limousine."

A Double Shot at Survival

Greg Weeks is a late bloomer when it comes to believing in miracles. An alcoholic once diagnosed with a fatal form of skin cancer, Greg never expected a miracle to save his life. Instead, faced with a diagnosis that left him little time to live, Greg hit the bottle harder than ever.

But miracles are not reserved only for the sober. In fact, two of them occurred in Greg's life at the same time: his cancer suddenly and completely disappeared, and an inner voice led him to an Alcoholics Anonymous meeting that transformed his life. . . .

Greg Weeks often talks more about his painful struggle against alcoholism than his survival of a usually fatal form of skin cancer.

"I'm a double miracle," Greg says. "Not only did I survive cancer, I also won my struggle with alcohol."

His story begins almost eight years ago. He and his wife were prompted to move from Cincinnati, Ohio, to Greenfield, Massachusetts, by the offer of a better job.

"About a year after moving here, I came home from

playing basketball one night and realized that I had extra tissue under my arm," he says. A visit to his doctor's office confirmed his worst fears—the diagnosis was an often fatal form of skin cancer.

"By the time I had surgery a couple of weeks later, I had five or six golf-ball-sized tumors," he recalls. Greg was 38.

He emerged from surgery with a nearly useless right arm. "They had to remove so much tissue, it caused nerve damage," Greg explains. This impediment distressed Greg, an avid sports and outdoors enthusiast, even further.

"But that wasn't my biggest problem," he says. "My prognosis was extremely poor and there wasn't any secondary treatment for this type of cancer." He was told to expect a major recurrence of a tumor within a year. If that tumor targeted his liver, lung, or brain, "the show would be over rather quickly."

It was a dismal period in his life. "I did all the things that cancer patients have to do. Cancer suddenly changes all the rules. I wasn't very happy at that point, but I hadn't been happy for a long time."

He emphasizes his negative state of mind, blaming it for his heavy drinking and for the cancer that he eventually developed.

"I'd been an alcoholic most of my life—since I was 18-years-old or so. I'd never been able to come to grips with it.

"I did everything that most drunks do in their drinking and drugging careers. I'd been luckier than most in that I managed to make a life for myself. But it was not a very happy life.

"Basically, I wanted to die. Life for me at that point was just one long misery." He says his body readily complied with that death wish. "Our bodies are very obliging things, and I discovered that mine was more than willing to help me die."

Greg adds that his medical diagnosis gave him even more of an excuse to drink heavily. "It was a license for me to drink the way I had always wanted to drink."

Meanwhile, fearing for her husband's health, Greg's wife expressed her desire to have a child before he died. Two months later she was pregnant.

Greg continued to consult with other medical specialists about his condition, but the prognosis was always the same. Little else could be done for him. "I went to various medical centers along the east coast to explore other options, but I didn't fit into any protocols for different experimental therapies."

Eventually, Greg says a local physician who was a personal friend suggested that he undergo a six-month trial with the still untested drug called Interferon. "They had no idea how much of a dosage to give me," he says. "What patients get today is about a tenth of what I was given."

In February, Greg's wife gave birth to a boy. Greg continued to take large doses of Interferon, along with other drugs and alcohol.

The side effects of Interferon caused him to feel depressed. There was another source of his depression as well. "The single largest effect of mass consumption of alcohol is depression," he notes. "Needless to say, I got to be a very depressed person."

Greg soon became suicidal. "I was dying anyway, and I wanted to kill myself. I was a mess, wolfing down Interferon and other drugs with bourbon. It just goes to show how unreasonable human beings can be when we're in the throes of fear and despair."

However, he made another attempt to stop drinking, checking into a local detoxification center. A few months of sobriety followed. Then Greg fell off the wagon again.

"Throughout this time I, my doctors, and everyone who knew me were expecting me to develop a recurring major tumor and die. But nothing of the sort happened."

The fact that no new tumor had appeared failed to cheer him up. His drinking continued. "I was in utter despair, close to an all-time low," he recalls. "One night I told my family and friends that I was headed out to an AA meeting. Instead, I disappeared for eight months."

Greg drove back to Cincinnati and checked into a cheap hotel. There, he hooked up with old drinking buddies and "got back to drinking the way I wanted to. I tried to drink myself to death or wait for the cancer to finally do its job." Meanwhile, his wife had legally separated from him.

One morning, Greg decided to return home. "My plan was to get back and gradually drink myself to death, but at least I could visit my son once in a while."

Fate, however, had something else in store for him. Instead of hitting the bottle when he got home, Greg decided to attend an AA meeting. Then, after going to more AA meetings, he found his whole outlook on life changing. "I began to learn things about myself," he says. "I kept going to those meetings, and I haven't had a drink since."

Greg and his family got back together again, and his life continued to improve. He found work as a hospital aide in the detox center of the local hospital, and began a new career in computer programming. In addition, he purchased a new home.

Incredibly, his nearly useless right arm began to heal.

"Today I play a lot of basketball and do a lot of running. My right arm is pretty good, and I've got a decent 20-foot jump shot again," he quips. "Best of all, there's no sign of any cancer in my life."

Greg calls it miraculous and so do his doctors. The whole experience has caused him to lead a very spiritual life. "I do a lot of praying on a regular basis, I stay active with AA, my work suits me, and I spend a lot of time with my son. My wife and I are even in the process of adopting another child."

Holocaust Survivor Saved by Miracles

Shoshana David, a survivor of a Nazi concentration camp, is all too familiar with the horrors of the Holocaust.

A lecturer on medieval Jewish literature at New York City's Jewish Theological Seminary, she says that, although more than 50 years have passed, the terrifying memories of that ordeal still remain, sometimes troubling her dreams at night.

But not all of Shoshana's dreams are nightmares. There are other, more mysterious memories of those perilous days as well—dreams that remind her of the unusual series of miracles that helped keep her alive in the midst of so much suffering and death. . . .

"Every minute that you were alive in a concentration camp was a miracle," says New Yorker Shoshana David, recalling in an emotion-choked voice the painful memories of those nightmarish days.

In 1944 Shoshana, a teenage girl, was one of thousands of Lithuanian Jews who were rounded up and transported to the Stuthoff Concentration Camp in Danzig, Germany.

"You just can't imagine how it was," she says. "It was like being in the *Twilight Zone* where nothing seemed to make any sense. If you said 'Good morning' to a Nazi guard they would kill you because Jews were not considered human and weren't supposed to speak to them. If you didn't say hello, they killed you because you didn't show them any respect. How could you survive under such circumstances except by a miracle?"

A frail girl, sensitive and susceptible to colds, Shoshana says she considered herself the least likely candidate to endure the brutal conditions at the work camp. She recalls that hundreds of people at the camp died daily from starvation or exposure, or else were routinely killed in the camp's gas chambers.

In recollecting those times, she is particularly amazed at having survived that one particular day in 1945 when her captors decided that it was her turn to enter the gas chambers. How she managed to cheat death, she says, can only be explained with one word: "miracle."

But before she relates that story, Shoshana says she wants to talk about a series of other miracles that kept her alive even before she was deported by the Nazis to the concentration camp.

She recalls that the war was beginning to wind down at the time, and Russian troops were advancing toward Lithuania where Shoshana, separated from her parents, was forced to live with thousands of other Jews in a cramped, unsanitary ghetto.

"The Lithuanian and Ukrainian collaborators used to line the Jews up five in a row, and a Nazi officer would pick out who would be transported to concentration camps," Shoshana recalls. She explains that many Jews did not seriously resist selection because they believed that life at a work camp could only be an improvement over the conditions in which they were then living.

"No one knew what lay ahead of them," she says. "No one knew then about the gas chambers."

Call it instinct or, as she does, a miracle, Shoshana remembers feeling as if "an eye watched over me." While some Jews pushed forward to the front row, the teenager always stood as far back to the rear and as far out of sight as possible.

"I don't know how to explain it. It was as if there was a hand pushing me toward the back of the rows of people. I just don't know why I kept going to the back, not wanting to be selected."

She talks emotionally about the many atrocities that Jews in that ghetto suffered. The Nazis' underlying plan, she says, was always to murder as many Jews as possible.

"Every day people were killed or simply vanished. The ghetto kept getting smaller and smaller. There would be a knock on the door—sometimes in the middle of the night—and people were pulled out of their beds for 'punishment.'"

She recalls that "our room was right on the main street. They would open doors in the building and pull people out to be punished for accepting bread, or for any other reason. But nobody ever opened the door where we were living. That was also some kind of miracle. They would come early in the morning and open all the doors to the other rooms in the house—but not ours."

Shoshana says she managed for three years to avoid the fate that befell so many of her neighbors and friends—death or deportation.

"I don't know why. I just never fell into either category. It was amazing—a miracle. An eye was watching over me, and a hand was leading me."

When word reached the dwindling number of Jews that Russian troops were quickly advancing, Shoshana remembers a surge of joy and excitement.

But that joy was short-lived when it was learned that the Nazis had decided to completely eradicate the ghetto, to leave no evidence behind of their inhumane treatment of the Jewish population.

This is when Shoshana says another miracle occurred.

"The Nazis had called in a special squad to destroy the ghetto," she recalls, anger rising in her voice at that memory. "Many of the Jews—including ourselves—had dug bunkers to try to hide. The squad brought dogs with them to sniff out the Jews who were hiding."

She says that if the Jews didn't immediately emerge from their bunkers, the Nazi soldiers would casually lob hand grenades into the house, killing everyone who was hiding there.

"But when they approached our house they asked us to come out. It was astonishing. They knew we were hiding, and they didn't throw in any hand grenades. They asked us to come out. I have no idea why."

Today, Shoshana speculates that one reason why she and her group weren't killed was because of their young ages. Although the Nazis were retreating from the Russian advance, they needed a labor force to build defenses that were necessary to protect them from the approaching army.

There is also another possibility to which she gives equal weight: a miracle.

Within a few days, Shoshana and the other women in town were on a freight train headed for the Stuthoff Concentration Camp, a German labor camp for women.

This is where Shoshana resumes her story of the greatest miracle that was yet to happen to her: the day she was miraculously saved from the gas chamber.

Shoshana says she knew her luck had finally run out when she and a group of other women were ordered to take a shower.

"They said they wanted to delouse us, but we knew that there were gas chambers in there. We knew that we would be killed and our bodies put in ovens to be burned. We saw chimneys smoking all day and smelled bodies burning."

Shoshana continues, "We had taken off our clothes and were waiting and waiting to go into the showers. Finally, the guards said, 'Let's go.' We closed our eyes and walked into the gas chamber."

The women were split into two groups. The first group entered the shower room, and were never seen again. Then it was her group's turn.

"We went in and we were waiting and waiting for the

gas. But something happened. The gas wasn't working." To their surprise, water came spurting out of the shower heads instead of gas.

For Shoshana, even to this day, it was the ultimate miracle in her life. Instead of death, she and the other women experienced nothing more than the chill of an ice-cold shower. Again, some mysterious force had somehow managed to keep her alive.

She says the women were then ordered back to their barracks and never again returned to the gas chamber. Instead, they were sent out to the fields to build defense fortifications.

"They left us alone. We spent a whole year there working in the fields and living in tents. It was bitter cold, not like the winters in the United States, and we had no winter clothes and very little food. Women were dying from the cold and starvation."

Shoshana survived that ordeal, as well—yet another miracle, she says. "Everything that happened to me was a miracle, even this. All I had to keep me warm was a dress and wooden shoes. The only blanket I had was one to sleep on. There was little to eat and a lot of women died of starvation. I was as skinny as a board but I survived."

The camp was eventually evacuated and its inmates were sent on a forced march away from the Russian army. Hundreds of women perished on that "death march." But again, she survived.

"It was miracle after miracle that saved me. It's a miracle that I survived and am telling you this story today. . . ."

AIDS and Cancer Victim Defies the Odds

When he was diagnosed with full-blown AIDS and two forms of terminal cancer, the Reverend Steve Peters, Director of the AIDS Ministry for the Metropolitan Community Churches in Washington, D.C., was given a slim chance of survival.

Thirteen years later, however, he has proven all the medical experts wrong. Today, the Reverend Mr. Peters remains active and healthy, with all his disorders in complete remission.

While the 42-year-old minister has no doubt that his survival is a miracle, he is not entirely satisfied. He seeks a greater miracle—one that will help more people than just himself. He is praying for a miracle that will bring about a cure for AIDS....

The Reverend Steve Peters's HIV symptoms first began to develop in 1982, while he was a pastor at the Metropolitan Community Church in Hartford, Connecticut.

Back then, however, HIV was still a relatively unknown virus, so Steve attributed his symptoms to burnout. The muscular, mustachioed minister decided to relocate to

Los Angeles, where he could slow down a bit and be with friends living there.

The move did not help his physical condition. "I got very, very sick when I got to Los Angeles," the minister recalls. By then, AIDS was a topic of discussion within the gay community. "I became very scared that I was coming down with AIDS, which people were now talking about."

There were no tests available at that time to detect the HIV virus, and Steve was told by a doctor who examined him that he did not have AIDS. Additional tests could not pinpoint what was wrong with him.

The minister, who is affiliated with the Universal Fellowship of Metropolitan Community Churches, says that "A lot of people didn't believe that I was really sick. Even members of my own church ignored me. It was a very difficult period in my life."

He soon was so ill that he couldn't leave his apartment. Only a next-door neighbor was available to assist him.

"She took care of me, brought me groceries and kept me company. I can't remember all the things she did for me, I was so blown away by what was happening to me."

Steve remained homebound through most of 1983. The following year, he felt much better. But not for long. His condition worsened and he was referred to L.A. County Hospital, where more tests were conducted. It was there that he met Dr. Alexandra Levine, who continues to be his physician to this day.

"She thought I had a benign swelling of the lymph glands, a condition that only in a small number of cases led to AIDS." The news gave Steve a bit of hope—until the results of additional tests came in. It was then that the minister learned he was gravely ill. He was 32 years old and suffering from terminal cancer.

More bad news followed. Doctors found a second type of cancer, along with symptoms of the HIV virus. When he asked his physicians how long he had to live, the answer was no more than a year.

This is when Steve believes the first miracle in his life occurred. "Something happened to me when they diagnosed me as terminal. When they told me in 1984 that I was not going to see 1985, something inside of me snapped and I decided that I needed to start doing everything I could to extend my life."

Steve's immediate goal was to live long enough to see a cure for AIDS. He chuckles at that thought now. "I was naïve enough back then to think that, 'Oh, sure, if I just manage to stay alive a couple of years or so, they'll find something to cure me.'"

He began to read all he could find about people who had beaten cancer. "There was nothing written about AIDS then, so I couldn't read about that. There were no longtime survivors, there were no treatments, and doctors told me there was nothing they could do to help me. There was no medication or anything for me."

He also began to explore alternative medicine. "I found there were a lot of people talking about beating some forms of cancer that were thought to be unbeatable in previous decades."

Soon he was developing a personal health-building program. It incorporated everything from laughter therapy and bodybuilding to prayer.

"I redoubled my efforts to get my body strong. I studied nutrition and vitamins very carefully. I took megadoses of vitamin C. I also did a lot of writing for my denominational magazine. I was the first minister to be diagnosed with AIDS and I wrote about that."

He also deepened his spiritual practices. "My faith certainly played a large part in my determination to survive. I preached the Easter service only two weeks after I was diagnosed as terminal. That really was tremendously important to me."

To his doctors' surprise, Steve was still alive when 1985 rolled around. Meanwhile, he continued his health-rebuilding program. "I quit smoking. I did everything I could to create the conditions of healing."

He gives credit to Dr. Levine for encouraging his efforts. "She told me that if I wanted the medicine to work when it came along, I would have to take care of my body. So I did—with nutrition, body building, laughter therapy, meditation, and visualization."

In January 1985, a new AIDS drug called Suramin was developed, and the clergyman was asked to become the first HIV-infected person to try it. "I agreed to do that. It was a heavy decision to give my body to science."

The immediate results were astonishing. "Six weeks after starting treatment—May 30, 1985—Dr. Levine called me and said, 'The drug worked. We've successfully repressed the HIV in your system and your cancers have gone into complete remission.'"

Steve laughs as he remembers that moment. "I wanted to shout from the rooftops and tell everybody that we found the answer." Doctors, however, cautioned him it was too early to celebrate. They said that for the drug to be pronounced successful, other patients had to experience the same results. Unfortunately, not many did.

Not long afterward, Steve again fell ill—this time as a result of undisclosed side effects of the powerful experimental drug. His voice is edged with a touch of bitterness as he recalls that setback. "The drug blew out my adrenal glands. We didn't know that adrenal deficiency was one of the side effects."

He pauses before continuing. "I came within inches of death before they could figure it out. All of us who were on Suramin were wasting away."

The minister describes this brush with death as a very profound, life-altering experience. "Even though I had, in reality, been facing death for a year and a half at that point, this was a real blow."

Eventually he recovered and began taking Suramin again. But when test trials for the drug ended in failure, it was removed from the market and he went without it.

Steve immediately developed severe medical problems, including paralysis on the left side of his body. He became temporarily blind and lost all his hair. Even more devastating, new tests indicated that he had reverted back to HIV-positive because he no longer had the Suramin to suppress the effects of the virus. "Everybody around me thought I was dying. So did I."

He continued to battle back, amazingly winning one small medical victory after another. "At one point I was terribly constipated. When that condition cleared, I began to feel better. I fought one battle at a time, and I began to recover."

And he has been feeling well ever since.

There's a long pause as the minister allows the impact of his story to set in. Then he goes on:

"I'll be the first to tell you that I don't understand why I've survived while so many others have not.

"It's a miracle that I could be diagnosed with full-blown AIDS and two types of terminal cancers and have it all go into remission at the same time. That is truly miraculous."

Steve, who has written a book about his experiences called *I'm Still Dancing* (he practices all forms of dance from tap to ballet), says that his wish is to share the miracle of his survival with millions of other AIDS victims.

"And, I'm praying for the greatest miracle of all," he says, "that a cure for AIDS quickly be found."

The Ski Glove That Saved Lives

Brett Woods's parents had almost decided not to buy him the expensive pair of ski gloves he asked for as a Christmas present because he had a tendency to lose things.

But Brett nearly lost something more than ski gloves when he and a friend were caught in an avalanche and trapped for nearly seven hours under a hillside of snow.

Today, Brett says he is more than grateful that his folks changed their minds about buying him the gloves because they turned out to be a heaven-sent gift. One of those gloves—along with some mysterious strangers—helped to save his life. . . .

Carolyn and Terry Woods of Durango, Colorado, were not particularly pleased when their son, Brett, then 19 years old, told them he wanted an expensive pair of blue canvas ski gloves for a Christmas gift. Brett, after all, had a habit of always losing his gloves and sunglasses, and they thought that buying such an expensive present would be a waste of money.

But at the last minute, Carolyn, an X-ray technician, and her husband, Terry, a Colorado state patrolman, decided to make the purchase anyway. After all, it was Christmas and their son really wanted the gloves.

Brett recalls how delighted he was when he opened his Christmas gift. "They were exactly the kind of gloves I wanted." Little did he know that the very next day one of those gloves would save his life.

Brett, 30, who today works as a salesman for a backpack company in Golden, Colorado, begins his story by talking about miracles.

"I was pretty lucky to be rescued the way I was. The whole situation was kind of miraculous. It happened on Christmas in a college town where all the students had gone home to celebrate the holiday. Yet somebody just happened to be walking around and I was able to get their attention."

Brett's ordeal began when he and a friend, 20-year-old Keith Cathcart, decided to go for a brief afternoon hike along a nearby hill. Keith would be having Christmas dinner with Brett's family, and the two pals felt the exercise would whet their appetites for the huge meal Brett's family planned for that evening.

As Brett and Keith were crossing the hill, the snow suddenly broke loose under their feet, and they found themselves in the midst of an avalanche.

"Hold on!" Keith shouted as he grabbed his friend. Together, they rode the avalanche down to the base of the hill, which was located only 15 feet from the roadway. They thought they were lucky—until they felt a second avalanche hit. It buried them completely in a vault of hard-packed snow.

The two friends were wedged in tightly, Brett positioned almost on top of Keith. Brett says he panicked at first. "I felt I was going to suffocate."

But he was able to poke his hand through the snow toward the surface, "and that kind of left my body free. The snow was still filling up around me, but I was able to make an air pocket."

Thinking back, he remembers how frightened he was at the time. Today, however, he chuckles as he tells his story. "We were packed in as tightly as two guys can ever get," Brett quips. "Keith was actually below me. My heel was in the palm of his hand. I couldn't see him, but we could kind of yell at each other, that's all. Keith was able to breathe the air that I got from the air pocket."

The surface was just out of Brett's reach. He couldn't break through the snow enough to extend his hand. Then he remembered his Christmas present. He pulled the left glove off with his teeth and tried to poke the stiff, thickly padded fingers up through the snow's crust. He failed.

Again and again he pushed the glove up over his head with his free hand, until he finally managed to get just the fingers of the glove wedged above the snow's surface. Although he knew the college town was virtually deserted because of the holiday, he prayed that somebody would happen to be passing by and see the blue canvas glove sticking out of the ground.

Despite the warm clothing the two men were wearing, hypothermia began to set in—a condition when all bodily functions are dangerously slowed down through exposure to extreme cold. This produces a desire to sleep, which slows the body down even more and can prove fatal.

"We slept for most of the time," Brett recalls. "Then I'd wake up and say, 'Oh, I haven't made any progress,' and I'd fall back asleep again. It was the lack of oxygen and the hypothermia."

Then what Brett believes was a miracle occurred. "I thought I heard something, and I could swear it sounded like footsteps." Was it possible at this time of day in a deserted area that someone just happened to be walking about? He listened again. Yes! It was footsteps! Brett began yelling for help.

He later was told that some people going by heard what sounded like muffled voices. When they walked up the hill to investigate, they spotted something small and blue against the snow—the fingers of Brett's blue canvas glove.

"To this day, the people who rescued us never have identified themselves," Brett says. "It's pretty odd. I don't know who would be walking around in that kind of cold weather. All I know is that they started digging us out."

Brett doesn't remember any of this, but was later told that the mysterious rescuers flagged down a passing car and even warmed up the two teenagers in the car until help came. He says they didn't even give their names to the police. "All I can remember after getting out of the snow is being in the ambulance."

Were Brett's rescuers possibly angels? Brett doubts it, but his mother takes a different view. "Ever since my children were babies I've said a prayer every night asking the Lord to watch over them. He always has, and I really feel this was one of those moments.

"The doctor told us that if they had been in the cold for another half hour, they would have died. It was a miracle that they were found. The Lord really was looking out for those boys that night. I think he sent somebody to find them."

Brett and Keith were released from the hospital within a week. Neither of them suffered anything more serious than frostbite on a few fingers and toes.

Brett, meanwhile, says he continues to be an outdoorsman. "I really like the outdoors, but I'm a little more careful about the snow. . . ."

A Mysterious Blessing Brings a Miraculous Birth

Sarah is a biblical name that is often associated with the miracle of birth. According to the Old Testament, the wife of Abraham miraculously conceived her son, Isaac, when she was 90 years old.

Sarah Abrams, wife of former New York State Attorney General, Robert Abrams, was not quite the ripe old age of her namesake when she decided to have a second child. However, doctors told her that, at age 46, she had less than a five-percent chance for a successful pregnancy.

But what the doctors and Sarah didn't quite expect is what some people have described as a miracle. It began with a blessing from a holy man and ended nine months later with the birth of a seven-pound, ten-ounce healthy baby girl. . . .

For anyone who is acquainted with modern-day Judaism's various religious denominations, the name Rabbi Menachim Shnearson is probably a familiar one. Until his death in 1994, Rabbi Shnearson was the revered leader of the worldwide, ultra-orthodox Hasidic sect known as the Labuvachers.

When Sarah and Robert Abrams met Rabbi Shnearson in 1973, they had just become engaged. The two young attorneys were introduced to the charismatic religious leader by a mutual friend who worked closely with the rabbi.

"He used to see people in the middle of the night," Sarah recalls. "We had to wait an hour or two to see him. We finally got to meet him, and from that time on we struck up a friendship with Rabbi Shnearson."

More than a decade passed, and their friendship with Rabbi Shnearson blossomed. Each year, usually around the Jewish High Holy Days, the Abrams would visit the rabbi at his world headquarters in the Crown Heights section of Brooklyn. Rabbi Shnearson enjoyed his talks with Sarah and her husband, often encouraging Robert's political ambition to run for the New York State Attorney's Office.

"We were hoping at a certain point to have another child," Sarah recalls, "and went to see a specialist. My first daughter, Rachel, was 10 years old at the time. The doctor we saw specialized in women who wanted to give birth at an older age. She told me that I had less than a five-percent chance of having another child."

Sarah, then 46 years old, was disappointed at the prognosis. Robert, however, adopted a different attitude. "My husband is the kind of person who doesn't give up easily, so we went to see another doctor. We didn't tell anybody what we were doing." But the result was the same. The second doctor also felt Sarah had little chance of conceiving a second child.

In September 1985, Sarah and her husband were returning from the funeral of a friend when they decided to pay a visit to Rabbi Shnearson.

He served the Abrams traditional holiday cake, then, with what Sarah remembers as an amused smile, made an unexpected proclamation that stunned the couple. "I give you a blessing for an addition to your family."

Sarah's jaw dropped. No one knew of the couple's desire to have a second child except for two doctors. Yet, somehow, Rabbi Shnearson was aware of their innermost secret.

"I'll never forget the conviction in his voice," she says. "His words came out of the blue. It took our breath away. How had he known?"

The rabbi's words made a deep impression on Sarah. "I carried the image of the rabbi giving us this blessing in my mind." Six weeks later, Sarah learned that she was pregnant.

On July 31, 1986, at age 48, Sarah gave birth to a healthy baby girl weighing seven pounds and ten ounces.

Two months later, on the Jewish New Year, the Abrams introduced their new daughter, Becky, to Rabbi Shnearson.

When Rabbi Shnearson looked at the child, he said, in almost the exact words that he had spoken to the couple the first time, "I see this as the addition to your family."

Sarah says the repetition of those familiar words shocked her husband. "The rabbi saw and talked to thousands of people, yet he repeated nearly the same exact words.... It was as if he were reminding us of his blessing, and the power that blessings contain...."

Prayer Puts Paraplegic Back on His Feet

After spending 21 years confined to a wheelchair, 53-year-old Army veteran Karlton Robinson thought he would never walk again. But that was before the Redwing, Minnesota, man turned to prayer as a way to overcome his disability.

Karlton says his newfound faith paid off. On a June morning, he left the Minneapolis Veterans Administration Center Hospital, where he had been undergoing rehabilitation, on his own two feet. . . .

Karlton Robinson is no stranger to serious injuries. Three times the muscular ex-soldier broke his back—twice in traffic accidents and once falling off a roof. Each time he made a full recovery.

The fourth time, however, he wasn't so lucky. He had been drinking and driving when his third car accident took place. His back was broken and he was paralyzed from the waist down.

Karlton lay unconscious in a Veterans Administration hospital for six months after his accident. When he finally regained consciousness, he had lost his memory and had to learn everything all over again—even the names of his family members.

Doctors told the veteran that he would have to be confined to a wheelchair for the rest of his life. Although some feeling eventually returned to his legs, Karlton thought they would be useless forever.

Devastated, the wheelchair-bound Minnesota man went about trying to put the pieces of his life back together. "I never really put my faith to any great test. I never hoped to walk. I just took it one day at a time," he recalls.

Nearly 21 years later, Karlton made a new friend who would dramatically change his life. Her name was Kathy Rickey, and she was deeply religious. "She'd come over and read the Bible to me. We'd talk about Jesus and miracles and all kinds of things."

Karlton told the woman what doctor after doctor had said about his condition—that he would never walk again. But Kathy disagreed.

"She was the one who got me to fully believe in the Lord Jesus Christ, and accept that He could perform miracles for me." Karlton's husky voice wavers with emotion as he remembers those moments. "She even had her pastor come over and pray with me."

Karlton says he not only became deeply religious, but gradually became convinced that someday he would walk again.

In June 1994, as a result of another ailment, Karlton checked into the Minneapolis Veterans Affairs Medical Center. The doctor who examined him gave the veteran some surprising news. The doctor thought that, with proper therapy, Karlton might walk again. "I was completely surprised at what he told me. I asked him, 'Why didn't you tell me this 20 years ago?'"

The doctor told Karlton that he was a different man now. His state of mind had changed. With Karlton's impressive upper body strength and good spirits, he had enough left in his legs for therapies to build on.

What Karlton believes to this day, however, is that a miracle had occurred in his life.

The Army veteran began five months of extremely rigorous therapy, determined that he was going to walk out of the hospital. Much of the therapy was painful, but Karlton kept assuring the medical staff that he could take it. "I would say, 'Stretch my legs further.'" He was eventually given the nickname "Rambo" by another patient who was impressed by his courage.

In the meantime, Karlton says he continued to participate in intensive prayer sessions. He prayed for his legs to work again so that he could walk.

One Friday afternoon, Karlton put his faith to the ultimate test and tried to leave the hospital on his own two legs. With the help of his physical therapist, the Army veteran took his first tentative step in front of a battery of television news cameras. The effort failed, and he fell to the ground. "In those moments that I was laying there on the floor, I prayed to Jesus to help me walk."

Even then, Karlton kept his sense of humor. From his awkward position on the floor he smiled up at the crowd of concerned reporters who had gathered around him. "Cut!" he yelled, causing laughter in the room.

Then he tried a second time.

With the help of his physical therapist, the Army veteran pulled himself off the hospital floor and back into his wheelchair.

Next, Karlton planted his feet firmly on the ground and again pulled himself upright from his chair. This time the results were different. With the help of a walker and leg braces, he took his first big step in 21 years. Karlton slowly strode down the VA lobby as smiling medical staff members followed. He went through the hospital door to the hospital grounds, where he was greeted with cheers from friends and relatives. Standing among them and applauding wildly was Kathy Rickey, the woman who had predicted this very miracle and encouraged Robinson to place his faith in God.

"It was all the result of prayer," he says. "I couldn't walk until I asked Jesus to get me walking again. It's a miracle after 21 years to be walking again."

And he promises a second miracle in the not too distant future.

"They say I won't walk my way out of these braces, but I said, 'You don't know me. It may take me a couple of years, but I'll get there.' The braces are good—they got me started—but they're not good enough...."

Miracles on the Airwaves

The Reverend Paul Keenan, host of a Saturday night radio program in New York City, has broadcast his fair share of inspirational programming since the show has been on the air.

But the Catholic priest says he has been receiving something quite remarkable in return.

It seems that each time a budget crunch threatens to cancel the financially struggling program, just the right amount of money turns up to keep it on the air. Based upon the show's remarkable survival, there must be Somebody tuned into the program who likes what He hears. . . .

Since 1992, the Reverend Paul Keenan has been fighting a constant battle of the budget to keep his show, "As You Think," on the air.

"The greatest miracle has been how things have worked out financially," the priest says. "We struggle from week to week to make the show work."

When things look the bleakest financially, something unexpected always happens to swell the show's coffers, he says. To illustrate that point, there's one anecdote he is very fond of relating.

"It was Thursday, and I was going over to my parish to give a talk. When I left the office here at noon, I was $1,000 short for the show that week.

"At the end of the talk a woman came over to me and said, 'Here's a donation for your program.' It was a check for exactly $1,000." The woman had no idea how much money he needed to keep the program on the air.

Father Keenan says this type of luck is "not something you take for granted. But you know that somehow God is working with us and is going to continue to do that."

He believes the show draws miracles because it helps the listeners: "We're really touching people's lives. We're helping them to know that, whatever the obstacles, there's something more to life than the problems that they face.

"The idea of the program is to provide a positive message for people—an inspirational message. There are so many negative messages that show up in people's lives. What I wanted was something that would give people a half hour of spirituality without preaching."

The audience response to the program, which airs on WOR Radio, has been overwhelming. It has also attracted popular personalities who appear on the program in support for the message Father Keenan is trying to get out to the audience.

"Our first guest when the program started in 1992 is another example of how the hand of God has been involved with this show," Father Keenan says. "It was former Disney star Annette Funicello. She was on just at the time that news of her muscular dystrophy was coming out.

"The actress turned down many requests for interviews," Father Keenan says, "but something about the way I presented my request caught her agent's eye. She said yes and was our first guest."

For a fledgling radio program with minimal name recognition, it was quite a coup to attract a star of her magnitude, Father Keenan says. But there's more to the story.

"In those days, we were on the air at 6:30 on Wednesday night, and this was our first show," he recalls. "It had been arranged that Annette was going to call us from California."

When the appointed time for the actress's phone interview arrived, there was no call. "So I went on the air and time was ticking away," he recollects. "Fifteen minutes passed, and still no Annette. I filled in and went to a break at 6:45. Finally, there she was."

Somehow Annette had been given the wrong telephone number. Instead of just canceling out on the interview, Father Keenan says, "She persisted, got the right number, and got through to us. I did the last 15 minutes of the show with her and she was delightful.

"There are really two kinds of miracles that operate in people's lives," Father Keenan explains. "First, there are the miracles that are well-known, like the miracles that happen at Lourdes and Fatima or other shrines."

But there are other miracles as well. "These are the unexpected, wonderful things that happen in people's everyday lives which can be explained only by the presence of God."

The Lord Taketh Away, *Then* He Giveth

There's an old saying that the Lord giveth and then taketh away. In Judy Carwile's case, however, it seems like the Maker decided to change the order of things a bit.

First, the 33-year-old Tampa, Florida, resident was in a serious automobile accident in which she suffered brain damage and lost her memory.

Little more than a year later, Judy was involved in a second car accident. But this time, Judy says a miracle occurred. Doctors discovered that the latest jolt had restored virtually all of her missing faculties...!

When Judy Carwile was injured in a car accident in upstate New York, the shaken woman was taken to a local hospital emergency room. There, doctors treated her for bruises, and, after examining her, they found nothing more seriously wrong with her.

About a year later, she was making plans to relocate to Florida, where a new job as a benefits coordinator awaited her. After her move, however, she began to experience allergy attacks and decided to visit a specialist.

When Judy described her symptoms to the neuropsychologist, including feeling "very spacey" and "very confused," he suspected something else was wrong. The specialist decided to test her for brain damage.

When the test results came in, Judy learned that she had sustained more damage in the accident than first suspected. She was experiencing symptoms of mild brain damage.

For the attractive, athletic brunette, it was devastating news. "I had a master's degree and all the credentials of someone with high intelligence. Now I was often forgetful, and my short- and long-term memory were affected."

Other problems related to her injury also developed. She now had difficulty following what people were saying to her, and experienced a personality change. Ordinarily calm and happy, she quickly became irritable over the smallest remarks.

What distressed her the most, however, was losing much of her creativity. "I used to be very good at assessing situations and coming up with ideas to resolve them. I was no longer able to creatively resolve problems, which was a very important part of my job."

After a year of treatment, the neuropsychologist told her she would simply have to learn to live with her reduced mental facilities and that, "Maybe in 20 years, your abilities will come back."

Judy was devastated but continued her therapy. "I learned how to teach my brain to think differently and did the best I could with what I had left after the accident. I adjusted my entire personality to work without the abilities that I had before.

"I was like the absentminded professor," Judy laughs. "I had a master's degree and was once really bright, but that wasn't there anymore. I had developed a whole different personality."

One thing Judy never lost, however, was her faith in God. "I knew there was a reason that I was walking around like this, although I didn't know what it was." She continued to pray for a complete recovery.

A week after her therapy ended, she was involved in a second automobile accident while returning home from work. A car ran a stop sign and broadsided Judy's car on the driver's side. "I thought, 'Oh, my God, more of my abilities are going to be taken away.'"

In despair, Judy returned to her doctor's office, where she again went through tests to see how much more damage was done.

Judy was in for a big surprise. "The tests came back normal. Almost every one of my abilities was back to normal."

She was overjoyed at the news. The miracle she had prayed for had occurred! "I know it was a miracle. All the objective tests and several doctors told me that I was permanently brain damaged. Then all my faculties and my personality were given back to me. I think that's miraculous."

She also believes her experience has improved her job performance, explaining that it has made her much more sympathetic to her clients.

"As a benefits coordinator, I deal every day with people who are suffering from illnesses and accidents. All this has helped me to be a better person and to help those people a little more."

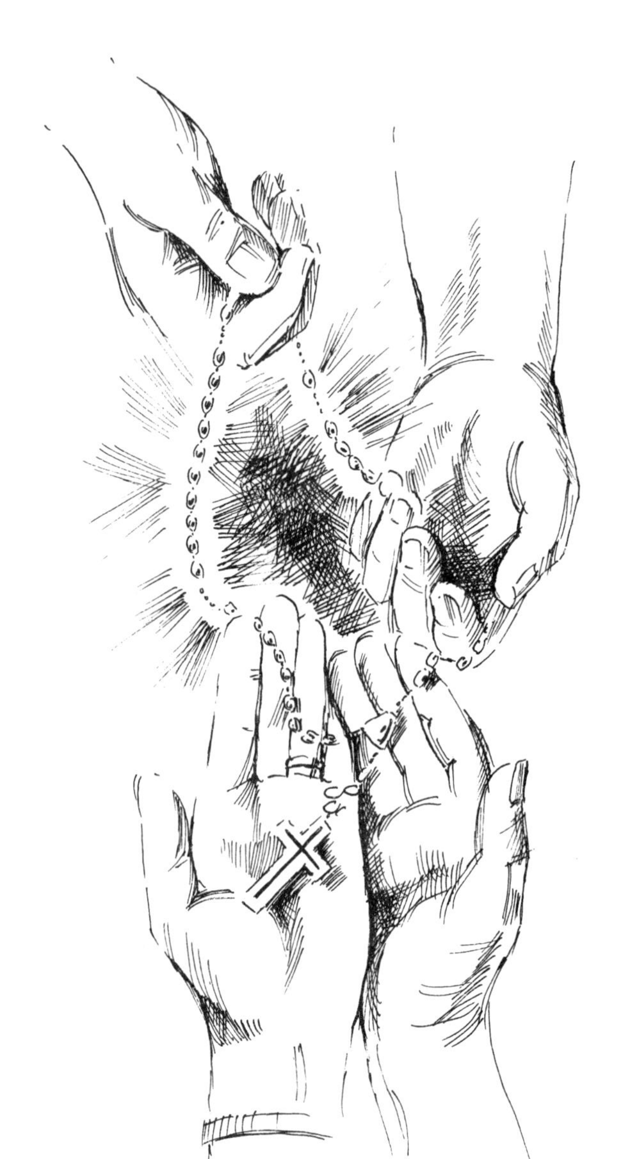

Visits from the Virgin Mary

Linda Russo, a worker in New York Hospital's Burn Unit, says she has twice been visited by the Virgin Mary. For many, this might be a startling statement. But Linda has more than just her word to prove her claim.

First, there's the mysterious photograph taken of Linda at a party. Many people who have examined the photo—including several priests—agree that an image of the Virgin Mary appears to be standing next to Linda.

Second is a string of rosary beads that Linda says turned gold—right before her eyes and those of a friend—while they were on a religious pilgrimage to a shrine of the virgin!

Still have your doubts? All Linda can say is, examine the evidence, and perhaps you'll change your mind. . . .

Religious miracles aren't often known to take place at a dog's birthday party. But if the Lord and His heavenly family work in mysterious ways, that's exactly where the first wonder took place for Linda Russo, a 42-year-old New York City mother of one.

"My friend Gary was having a birthday party for his dog," Linda recalls. "It was a fun party. I bought Gary a present—a relic of St. Jude."

Linda explains that St. Jude is the patron saint for hopeless cases, and Gary was having a lot of problems with his career at that time.

"He's an artist and in sales, and he wants to do things with his life. But he wasn't getting anywhere and he was fed up," she says.

She recalls that, upon presenting Gary with her gift, he burst into tears. "It cost only 87 cents, but he started crying, telling me it was the most beautiful and thoughtful gift anyone had ever given him."

In return, Gary gave Linda a watercolor painting he had recently finished. Once the gifts were exchanged, Linda began taking pictures at the party. She asked Gary to take one of her, never expecting the results that would change her life.

"I brought the camera over to the store to have them develop the film," she says. "It was a roll with 24 pictures on it. I never took it out of the camera."

When Linda picked up the prints a few days later and looked at them, she couldn't believe her eyes.

"I looked at one of the pictures, then I looked at it again," she recalls. "There was a picture of the Blessed Mother standing next to me. It wasn't a statue, but a white apparition as big as a person and standing on a cloud. She was almost as large as one whole side of the photo."

Linda's first reaction was to find out if someone at the camera store had played a practical joke on her. She returned to the store to question the manager.

The manager looked at the print and immediately agreed that the image on the photograph did resemble the Virgin Mary. But he also told Linda he thought exposure to light had created the image.

"He said, 'Oh, you must have opened the camera,'" she recalls. "I said, 'I never opened the camera.' He said, 'That's the only way this could have happened.'"

Convinced that there was a more miraculous explanation, Linda showed the print to her local priest. "He said, 'It's definitely the image of a woman, but I'm not going to say it's the image of the Blessed Mother.'"

But when a woman working in the parish office looked at the photograph, the woman began to shout, "My God, it's the Blessed Mother! It's the Blessed Mother! It's the Blessed Mother!"

This attracted the attention of other women working in the office who, upon looking at the photograph began shouting, "It's the Blessed Mother!"

At New York City's St. Catherine of Sienna Church, Linda finally received the confirmation she was seeking. The church's 76-year-old priest, the Reverend Patrick Connolly, took one look at the photograph and told her without hesitation, "This is definitely the Blessed Mother."

"Father Connolly's an old-fashioned, strict priest," Linda says. "He wouldn't say this to placate me."

Soon afterwards, Linda showed the photograph to a priest at Our Lady of Peace Church. He also agreed that the image resembled that of the Virgin Mary.

Now firmly convinced she wasn't imagining things, Linda began to wonder why the Holy Mother had appeared to her in such a peculiar way.

"I've always had a lot of faith, but I still couldn't figure out why that image had appeared," she says. Then Linda had another experience. A second visit from the Virgin Mary convinced her there was, indeed, a purpose to her visitation.

Linda's second contact with the Virgin took place while she was on a pilgrimage to a farm near Conyers, Georgia, 30 miles east of Atlanta. Nancy Fowler, the farm's owner, is a 47-year-old homemaker to whom the Virgin Mary has reportedly appeared 16 times. Each year, thousands of people visit her farm.

It was there, in October 1994, that Linda had her second miraculous experience.

When Linda and her friend, Luzmania Londono, arrived at the farm, they decided to view the room where the apparition had been seen. They stood in a long line with hundreds of other pilgrims waiting to see the shrine. "The line kept moving. Finally, Luz and I had to make one turn and we would be inside the house."

As they approached the entrance of the house, Linda says her friend suggested that they pray before entering the apparition room. Linda agreed.

"I reached into my bag and opened up a box where I had kept a very special string of black prayer beads. They were more than 120 years old and belonged to my great-grandmother."

Linda was handing the beads to her friend when a miracle took place—one that neither of them will forget.

"I was placing the beads across her open palms, and it was as if somebody had taken a spray can of gold, and went up and down the beads," she recalls. "It was incredible. They were changing from black to gold very, very slowly right before our eyes."

Linda says the two women watched in fascination as the transformation took place. "It was unbelievable," she says. "Right there, a quarter of an inch off the beads, in the air, this gold spray was coming down like powder—like angelic dust. It went on the prayer beads and on Luz's hands."

"The first miracle is what happened, the second miracle is that we both saw it," Linda says. "This happened in broad daylight. We instantly got down on our hands and knees and began praying."

She says no one else witnessed the actual transformation of the beads, but when Linda turned to show them to a man and his wife standing in line behind her, "the couple became excited and were absolutely in awe. They didn't see it happen, but they saw the results."

Linda's first reaction was to think "it was a message that my great-grandmother was in heaven." Today, Linda believes that, along with the photograph, it was a reminder of her special calling.

"I believe the Virgin wants me to go on a mission to convert people—Christians and non-Christians alike. I think the photograph and the beads were given to me as tools to help me in my mission because I'm not a good speaker," she says. "What better proof than to be able to show people these things?"

The Woman Who Healed Herself

Guided meditation and creative visualization are unconventional techniques thought to bring about positive changes in health and mental well-being.

Perhaps no one can appreciate these methods more than Kathleen Burghardt. A consultant for the Florida State Department of Education, Kathleen used these techniques along with prayer to cure herself of a potentially life-threatening ailment.

Kathleen Burghardt's visit to her gynecologist in 1991 was a routine one. It was time, once again, for her yearly mammogram. Kathleen didn't anticipate any problems, so it came as a surprise to the 51-year-old consultant when her doctor called three days later, asking her to return for further testing.

The results of the second mammogram and ultrasound tests confirmed the worst. Two lumps were detected in her right breast. They were not fluid-filled cysts, but solid masses. Cancer was a distinct possibility.

Kathleen went to Fort Lauderdale's Imperial Point Hospital, where a biopsy was scheduled. "They were going to do a needle localization for a biopsy," she recalls, "but I became so ill when I looked at those needles that I fainted. I woke up with doctors, nurses, and orderlies all around me. My blood pressure had dropped, and I had scared them all to death."

Kathleen canceled the procedure and returned home. She decided not to have a needle biopsy. "I told them that if they were going to do a biopsy on me, they would have to do it without the needle procedure."

Six months passed. Upon the urging of her doctor, Kathleen returned to the hospital for new mammogram and ultrasound tests. The results were the same. There were still two lumps in her right breast.

For yet another six months, the Fort Lauderdale mother of two put off having a needle biopsy—or any other tests—performed on her.

"I was procrastinating and postponing it because I had known three people in three years who had died of breast cancer. They had mastectomies and they still died. I said I can't see going through all this mastectomy stuff and dying of cancer anyway."

Kathleen eventually consulted a religious counselor and confided her fears about undergoing surgery for breast cancer. The counselor sympathized but also urged Kathleen to undergo treatment. Still, she delayed doing so.

Kathleen says it was at that point that she decided to attend a lecture by Dr. Brian Weiss, former chairman of psychiatry at Miami's Mount Sinai Medical Center and author of *Through Time into Healing*.

"I read a best-selling book he had written, called *Many Lives, Many Masters*, about his experience with reincarnation. I thought that he might have something new to say about healing, something that I didn't know. I just knew that I had to see him."

Kathleen remained after the lecture and seized the opportunity to talk to the psychiatrist. She briefly explained her predicament and asked Weiss to take her on as a patient. "He said his practice was full and that he wasn't taking on any new patients, but suggested that I put myself on a waiting list." She did.

Six weeks later, Kathleen found herself seated opposite Weiss in his Miami office. The psychiatrist had agreed to see her on a short-term basis. Kathleen recalls feeling a bit skeptical at the time and somewhat frightened—not really knowing what to expect and worrying about the impact of his techniques on her religious beliefs.

"I told him that I was a Christian and that I wasn't into this New Age stuff, that I didn't want to open myself to anything Satanic," she recalls, mirth in her voice as she relates that conversation. "He looked at me like I really needed a psychiatrist."

Weiss assured her that nothing he recommended would be offensive to her religious beliefs. Then the psychiatrist reached for a tape recorder.

"He actually made a healing tape right in front of me on his tape recorder. He sat me in a chair and showed me how to do relaxation techniques, meditation, and visualizations. He showed me how to put healing light into my body."

Kathleen left Miami and returned to her Fort Lauderdale home. That Friday evening, she began practicing the techniques she had just learned. She frequently repeated the techniques over the weekend.

"I would close my eyes and picture a warm, bright, white healing light at the top of my head. I would focus on it and feel its glow and warmth. Next, I would slowly move the light from my head to my toes, letting it permeate every cell, organ, and artery before finally concentrating it on the part of me that needed the healing—my right breast. I would bathe the breast in that warm, glowing light. And I would end by picturing the light surrounding me from without and within."

Several days later, Kathleen agreed to return to Imperial Point Hospital for another mammogram. There was no difference in any of the tests. She was disappointed. "I said, 'OK, that does it. Let's have the biopsy.'" If necessary, she had decided to have her breast removed.

Although disappointed at the results of the mammogram, Kathleen continued to practice her guided meditation techniques.

On a Monday, almost one year from the day that she first received the disturbing news about her medical condition, an anxious Kathleen was back at Imperial Hospital being prepped for the dreaded needle biopsy. She remembers it was the day before Hanukkah, the Jewish festival of lights.

"The radiologist came in, looked at me, and looked at an X-ray he had just taken," she recalls. "He looked stunned. He said, 'I don't believe it. The lumps are gone.'"

The news was not only a surprise to her, but to the physicians who were treating her as well. "None of my doctors would acknowledge anything. They all said it was just one of those unexplainable things. But I knew differently. I knew that it was a miracle and that I had been healed. I knew it was a result of fasting and prayer and listening to those meditation tapes."

Despite the mysterious disappearance of the lumps in her breast, Kathleen's doctors still recommended surgery as a precautionary measure. She refused, but agreed to be X-rayed every three months. The results have always remained the same—a clean bill of health.

"It's all been documented at the hospital," she says. "I've been through additional mammograms and ultrasound testing and there's nothing there. It's been more than two years and I'm perfectly healthy. . . ."

Miracle on the High Seas

Whenever men go out to sea, there is always a risk that some of them will never return. Stories of the sea abound with sunken ships, drowned sailors, and doomed fishermen who leave their harbors never to be seen again.

There are also many extraordinary tales of survival on the high seas against difficult odds, and this is one of them. It's a Christmas story, of sorts, one that demonstrates the miracle of a mother's faith and the power of prayer. . . .

It began, as stories of miracles often do, just a few days before Christmas. Thirty-three-year-old Nick Lackey and his friend, Ernie, had decided to go crab fishing in the waters of the Pacific, about 150 miles north of San Francisco. Nick and Ernie were both seasoned crab fishermen, and Eureka Bay was familiar fishing ground.

What Nick hadn't expected was the fast-moving storm that kicked up, one in which gentle 10-mile-an-hour breezes suddenly turned to menacing gusts of 40 miles per hour within 20 minutes. He recalls that the southeaster slammed into *Blessed Redeemer*, their 38-foot boat, like a brick wall. Within five seconds, huge waves had flipped the boat completely over.

"A crash came out of the fo'c'sle and the boat rolled upside down," Nick recalls. "We just barely had enough time to get out of the cabin."

Nick and his boatmate found themselves immersed in turbulent, wind-slashed water. For nearly two hours they clung desperately to the overturned boat. Suddenly, two boxes surfaced from beneath the water—one of them large enough to serve as a flotation device. Nick spoke up first, urging his shipmate to swim to the box and save himself.

"Ernie got to the box and had drifted 250 yards away when, all of a sudden, the life raft popped up in its fiberglass canister," he recalls. "I dove in and got the life raft out of the canister."

Nick nearly drowned in the process. Huge waves slapped at him as he struggled to inflate the fragile life raft. When the raft was finally inflated, again Nick's first thought was of his friend. He pulled the sea anchor up on the raft and began paddling toward Ernie. But a 40-mile-per-hour gust of wind kept pushing him back, and he couldn't reach his friend.

"I had slowed the raft down about 75 feet from him," Nick remembers, "but the wind kept pushing me further and further away. It was dark and I could hear Ernie hollering, 'Help!' There was nothing I could do. It was the last I saw of him."

Nick now found himself all alone in the empty ocean. A bone-chilling night passed. Then another day. The raft began to leak. Huge waves would sometimes collapse the life raft and, at other times, tip it over. "I was numb all the time because of the cold, and I had to keep moving constantly," he recalls. There were moments when, exhausted and without food or water, he wanted to give up.

That kind of thinking never entered Elaine Lackey's mind. Nick's mother had learned about her son's boating accident from the Coast Guard, but she refused to believe that he had drowned. "I was sick with worry when it became evident that Nick's boat had sunk. But I felt that if my son was gone, I would be grieving—and I was not grieving."

Even when the Coast Guard, after a three-day fruitless search, declared Nick "presumed dead," Elaine says she felt that her son was still alive, but in grave danger.

"The third night after the storm—it was a Thursday—I tried to sleep for the first time," she says. "My husband and

I went to bed, and I resolutely closed my eyes. If I could just sleep, I told myself, the time would pass more quickly, and maybe there would be good news in the morning."

What happened when she began to doze off is something Elaine can't really explain, even today. "It was the middle of the night, and I felt as if I had been tossed up in the air. I grabbed the edge of the mattress and heard myself whisper, 'Hang on, Nick.'"

She remembers several times during the course of the night feeling as if she were being physically jerked around. "I would grab hold of the iron headboard to keep myself from falling onto the floor. Each time it happened, I cried out louder, 'Hang on, Nick!'"

Elaine's husband, in bed beside her, did not share her experience, but he felt his wife's distress. He tried to comfort her, but when she shut her eyes the phenomenon would resume.

"I tried to be quiet to let him sleep, but I was not in control," she says.

The tossing continued. It was as if Elaine, herself, were lost at sea and thrashing about in the dark, cold ocean: "The tossing became more violent, and I began to gasp and choke as if water had poured into my face and up my nose."

Elaine remembers that, after one particularly violent toss, "I found myself nearly upright, with my hands clenched tightly around the top of our iron bedstead, sputtering the 'water' out of my nose and mouth and yelling at the top of my lungs, 'Hang on, Nick!'"

Friends and neighbors soon heard that Nick was missing. Prayer vigils in Fort Bragg and adjoining areas were quickly established. If Elaine Lackey had not given up hope that her son was alive, neither had other people in the area.

Two days later, their prayers were answered.

On Christmas Eve, around noon, Nick weakly watched a Greek freighter called the *Fifth Avenue* steam by in the distance. The ship gave a sudden blast of its horn and Nick's heart leaped. The freighter had spotted his life raft! When he was picked up at Cape Blanco, Nick had drifted 150 miles from where his boat had first capsized—a fact that amazed his rescuers.

Nick was cold, dehydrated, and exhausted after spending five terrible days in the ocean without food, sleep, or drinkable water. He was so weak, he could barely make it up the ladder to the deck of the Greek freighter.

"There's no reason I should have made it through except for a lot of other people's faith," he says. "Thursday night was the hardest. The sea kept tossing the raft around, and the waves kept filling it with water. I had to keep bailing the water out. I heard someone calling my name—"Nick, Nick"—from out over the water. I heard it several times. Whether it was fatigue, or delirium or something else, I don't know."

What he does know, is that voice sustained him, along with the unwavering thought of wanting to return home to his wife and children for Christmas.

For Elaine Lackey, the return of her son was a real Christmas miracle. "I think it was a combination of prayer and the kind of psychic abilities I believe everyone is capable of," she says. "I just had great confidence that he would be found. . . ."

James Dean Returns to Tell His Story

Is the restless spirit of James Dean mysteriously in contact with a young woman who has devoted many years of her life to writing about the legendary actor?

Patricia A. Leone, who wrote and directed the 1993 off-Broadway production of "James Dean/ A Dress Rehearsal," will matter-of-factly tell you that is the case.

Patricia says it was Dean's spirit who encouraged her to pen the play about little-known facets of his life, and that he is now assisting her with a book she is writing about him.

She adds that the "Rebel Without a Cause" definitely has found one in the afterlife—to let his millions of fans around the world know who the real James Dean was. . . .

She is blond-haired, petite, attractive, and filled with a vast storehouse of little-known personal anecdotes about a young man who is still considered one of the greatest actors of all times, James Dean.

And Patricia A. Leone says that much of her information does not come from reading books about the late actor—who died tragically in a 1955 car accident—but from Dean's spirit, who she insists often uses her skills as a writer to tell his story.

"I think he died before completing things in his life that he wanted to complete," says Patricia, whose Greenwich Village apartment in New York City overflows with posters, paintings, and other memorabilia. "Many people knew all about his movies, but not much about who he was and what he was all about. He wants to get that known."

Patricia says that after Dean's fatal accident, thousands of his fans could not accept the fact that their screen idol was dead. "They thought he was maimed and that he was in an institution or a hospital," she explains.

She believes that Dean's spirit responded to that intense wish for him to be alive, so he is sticking around in spirit. "That's why nearly 50 years after his death he is more powerful and well-known today than when he was alive. All the continuing adulation keeps him earthbound."

Dean's spirit first made its presence known to Patricia more than a decade ago. Fresh out of school, she was seeking work as a theater director in Denver, Colorado.

"There weren't any directorial positions available, and I was asked if I wrote plays. I had experience writing in college so I thought that I'd write something."

Several weeks later, while dining with friends, Patricia had an inspiration to write a play about Dean. "It was just a thought. It wasn't as if the whole play came to me."

From that moment on, Patricia says she found herself almost obsessed with ideas for a play about the life of an actor she hardly knew anything about.

"Thought after thought about what to write about started coming to me. It was uncanny." Patricia eventually became so unnerved by the experience that she sought the opinion of psychics in the area.

"They told me that James Dean wants people to know who he really was, and he didn't have a chance to tell them. It was because of my decision to write about him that he seized the opportunity to come alive again."

Eight years later, Patricia's play opened to good reviews in an off-Broadway theater. "The play gave the audience a glimpse of what the real James Dean was all about. That was Jimmy's ambition."

Patricia says that most of the material she uses in writing about James Dean comes through spiritual channeling sessions. During these sessions she enters a deep trance state and receives information from another plane.

She cannot pinpoint the exact source of her information. "Whether it's James Dean, or another energy source who knows about him, I can't exactly say. What I find interesting is that much of the information that I've received through channeling over the years matches material in books about him that I've never read or looked at in my entire life."

She says Dean does not tolerate discouragement from those who are involved in projects about him. When Leone was unable to raise funds to produce her play in an off-Broadway theater, she nearly gave up her plans.

"There were times," she says, "when I thought about abandoning my efforts to see the play produced in New York City. But I couldn't because I was absolutely driven by him to see it through." She adds:

"When he's around and wants something to happen, like having a play or a book written about him, it always does. Everywhere I went, I would come across photos of Jimmy. I felt his presence telepathically. It was as if his voice were in my head at night encouraging me. Sometimes I'd feel his spirit in my apartment. His energy was everywhere."

Leone finally produced the play by investing money from her own savings. It did well, and she even managed to make a profit.

Patricia describes her new book about Dean as "very special." She says it contains things about the late actor's life that are not included in any other book on the subject—material that he wants his fans to know about.

"He's still around, and I feel his energy on an almost-daily basis. He's working with me on this project to have people understand him. It's just one of those unexplained miracles of life after death."

Man Dines with Family Hours After Being Shot!

Dan Blake believes it is nothing short of miraculous that he is still alive today, and he has very good reason for saying so. After all, how many people get shot between the eyes with a heavy-duty weapon and live to tell about it?

The Paso Robles, California, veterinarian is one of those people, the victim of a freak shooting accident. When the smoke cleared, not only had he survived the bullet wound, but just a few hours later he sat down to enjoy dinner with family and friends. . . .

On a pleasant Saturday afternoon, Dan Blake was hosting a family gathering on his farm. His nephew, Tom, was an avid gun collector, and the talk turned to that topic.

"Tom had just purchased a British Enfield rifle," Dan recalls. "He fired it a couple of days before, and the bullet had gone through steel. He was telling us how it could shoot through a half-inch plate of steel."

Dan said he wanted to see a demonstration of a rifle whose bullets could penetrate steel. The two men—joined by Dan's brother-in-law—found a half-inch plate of steel and propped it up against a tree stump.

"Then we paced off 60 feet," Dan recalls. "Tom took aim, while I stood behind him. I thought that I'd peek my head out a little bit, so I craned my neck to the right so I could watch."

Tom fired the powerful weapon.

"Bang! The gun went off and a split second later I felt like I had been hit between the eyes with a hammer," Dan remembers.

Incredibly, the bullet struck the metal and then ricocheted straight back, penetrating Dan's forehead.

"I remember thinking, 'Oh, my God, I've been hit in the head. How can that happen?'" He staggered back. Blood was spurting everywhere from a dime-sized hole located between his eyes.

"With all that blood I was sure I was going to die—that there was major brain damage," he says.

Family members rushed Dan to nearby Twin Cities Community Hospital. Throughout the ride, the 57-year-old veterinarian worried that he was going to bleed to death from all the blood that was still pouring from his wound.

But when he arrived in the emergency room and doctors treated him, they discovered no serious damage. The bullet had fractured Dan's skull, punching a hole in it, but his brain had not been harmed.

Doctors later explained that Dan had survived the gunshot wound because the bullet was slowing down when it struck the part of his forehead where two tough layers of bone protect the brain. The bullet had penetrated half an inch through the first bone layer and bounced off.

"A few days later, we went looking for the bullet and found it 15 feet from where I had been standing," he says.

Dan says when he entered the emergency room he had no idea how badly he was hurt. "But when the doctors told me there was no serious damage, they said they wanted to keep me overnight for observation. I told them, 'I want to go home.'"

The accident took place at 2:30 P.M. By 6 P.M., Dan was back home eating dinner with his family and their guests.

The veterinarian describes it as nothing less than a miracle that he is still alive.

"If the bullet had hit me an inch lower, it would have gone through my eye and hit the brain," he says. "Or if my head had been turned, it would have hit me in the temple."

Looking back, Dan describes the entire episode as a positive experience. He says he hasn't touched a gun since. "It was frightening, but the outpouring of cards and prayers has made it more positive than negative. I've thanked God more than once. I'm alive through His grace."

Housewife Becomes a Healer

Her hands have the gift of healing, and her mind is finely tuned to a world of spirits and other-dimensional beings that few of us have ever seen—let alone have the ability to communicate with.

Yet, for California spiritual healer Dolores Fairchild, it's all in a day's work, part of an extraordinary gift with which she has been blessed and that allows her to help others in need....

For more than two decades, psychic, medium, clairvoyant, and spiritual healer Dolores Fairchild has been using her unique psychic skills to help people.

It is a gift that the Davis, California, resident says she is blessed to have, but did not always possess. Until 1972, her life ran a rather ordinary course as a housewife who stayed home to raise four children.

Dolores clearly recalls the frightening and confusing day when all that suddenly changed: "It was December 21 in Sylmar, California, where I lived at the time. I was sitting in my living room, and I suddenly started seeing a lot of people and hearing a lot of voices."

The images baffled and frightened her. "I thought that maybe I had snapped something in my head. I didn't know what was going on."

The 58-year-old woman says the experience took her totally by surprise. She had never practiced meditation or expressed any interest in the world of the paranormal.

"I kept telling myself that I was not crazy. I was walking around my house, and everywhere I looked there were men in robes smiling at me, talking to me, and waving at me."

Dolores called a friend—a woman familiar with psychic matters. During that conversation, Dolores learned something about herself. Her friend told her that, according to Dolores's astrological chart, Dolores had always possessed psychic abilities, but they were just now unfolding.

Dolores devoted herself to learning more about her abilities. "I knew I had to learn more about what was happening to me. Otherwise, I probably would have gone out of control, and they would have locked me up! I learned control and how to deal with my powers."

She learned how to make contact with entities from beyond this world, and how to call upon them when their assistance was required in her healings—such as the miraculous healing of a man with a severe heart condition.

"He was being treated at the UCLA Medical Center for a heart condition," Dolores recalls. "His aortic valve was malfunctioning, and his charts had basically filled up a whole room." After being introduced to the man through a mutual friend, she began a series of healing sessions with him. During these sessions, Dolores used several different healing techniques to help the man. She used healing touch, which involved using her hands to shift healthy energy into the man's body; healing crystals; prayers; and kinesiology, a method of testing muscles to determine what is going on in the body.

"I worked with him twice a week for about a month. Each time he left our sessions he was feeling better, and he was able to decrease his medication. His health continued to improve, until he was completely off his medication."

Dolores says that when her client returned to the medical center for more tests, doctors were amazed at the improvement of his condition.

Dolores credits her spirit guides for assistance in this healing, as well as in her other healings. "I work with various teachers and guides. If I need someone with a knowledge of the human heart, I ask for one with those healing skills to assist me."

There is no doubt in Dolores's mind that spiritual guides such as those with whom she works really exist. "These guides and teachers are working through me. They tell me what to do and I do it. They channel their energy through me. It's definitely not my imagination."

While some people have described Dolores's healing skills as miraculous, she takes a more pragmatic view.

"I've been doing this so long that it's become normal and natural for me. Someone else may call it a miracle; I feel that I'm simply a channel and I've been given the gift to help."

The Track Star Who Ran for His Life

Since he was 16, Ohio State University track-and-field star Chris Nelloms has been a winner in his sport—breaking long-held records along the way. His prowess on the track, in fact, has earned him recognition as one of the world's top ten, up-and-coming young athletes in track and field.

Chris's biggest victory, however, came not on the track but in a hospital trauma unit, where he lay near death as a result of a gunshot wound.

Chris beat the odds in remarkable time and today is on the comeback trail, readying himself for the 1996 Olympic trials. He is alive, he says, only because a series of miracles saved his life....

Chris Nelloms believes that bad things sometimes happen to people because "good things are right around the corner, and God wants to make sure that you're aware and can handle the good things."

It's a philosophy that has served the 23-year-old Columbus, Ohio, college track star well—particularly since that tragic day in 1992 when he was shot by unknown assailants and nearly killed. Instead of slowing him down, Chris says the incident had just the opposite effect, filling him with more determination than ever before to win an Olympic gold medal.

Chris recalls that evening in detail. It was a warm August night, and he was at home watching the Olympics on television. He remembers feeling disappointed while watching the Games because he had qualified to compete in the preliminary trials, but was sidelined by a hamstring injury.

"Around midnight I decided to go for a seven-mile run," Chris recalls. "Whenever I'm upset, I run. It just makes me feel better."

It was almost the last sprint of his life. As Chris was returning home, shots suddenly rang out in the night. To Chris's horror, they seemed to be aimed at him! Then, one of the bullets struck him in the back.

"I remember falling down on the ground with blood gushing out of me," Chris says. That's when the first of two miracles occurred.

He found the strength to get up, but he discovered that his ordeal had just begun. "I got up, and one of the three guys who had the gun aimed it at me. But it didn't fire,"

Chris says. "I guess he ran out of bullets." The gunmen took off. "I got up and started running to my house, which made my heart pump blood faster," he says.

Chris collapsed to the ground for the second time, certain he was going to die. "I knew it was serious by the amount of blood coming out of me. The blood kept spurting out, and it was hard for me to breathe."

Which is when the second miracle occurred.

"I spread myself out and said, 'Lord, if it's time for me to go, I'm prepared to go. I know that I've lived my life right and have tried to do the things I could to become one of your angels.' I felt myself falling into unconsciousness."

Miraculously, as if in answer to his prayer, Chris says he suddenly felt a burst of new energy. "I regained consciousness, got up on both my knees, and crawled 400 feet to my house. It was no doubt a miracle that I could do all this."

Chris goes on to explain that the body holds 14 pints of blood; he was later told he had lost 10 pints even before arriving at the hospital. "It was a miracle that I was still alive when I got there," he says.

Once at the hospital, the athlete was rushed to the trauma unit, where he underwent surgery for nearly seven hours. Afterward, he was placed on a life-support system for three days. Incredibly, a week later he was released.

"Even that was pretty miraculous," he says. "I was supposed to be in the hospital at least a month. The doctor who did the surgery was amazed at my recovery.

"The doctors told me that the bullet exited the left side of my chest. It pierced my left lung and shattered my collar bone. I don't have any collar bone today. The bullet also severed the artery that pumps blood from the heart to the brain."

Chris later learned that, if the bullet had entered his body a centimeter closer to his heart, or if medical help had arrived five minutes later than it did, his life and career would have ended right there.

To this day, Chris cannot figure out who wanted to kill him and why. What mattered to him most was his future in track. He worried that the injuries might slow him down or, worse, keep him from competing altogether. Doctors assured Chris otherwise. They were right—soon, he was practicing again.

"The fifth day after intensive care I was already up and walking around. It was my brother who really encouraged me. He kept saying, 'Come on, we gotta get you ready for the Olympics.'"

It didn't take much encouragement to persuade Chris to pick up where he left off in his quest for a gold medal.

"I've done things that even Jesse Owens never accomplished. I won three gold medals in the junior world championship. No runner in the history of track and field has ever done that. A bullet wasn't going to slow me down."

He quickly proved his point. Just eight months after being released from the hospital, Chris won the 1993 Big Ten Indoor Championship in track. Two weeks later, he took first place in the NCAA Indoors Championship, followed by another victory in the Big Ten Outdoor Championship. Succeeding victories quickly established him as one of the 10 top track-and-field competitors in his division in the world.

Today, besides practicing for the upcoming Olympic trials, Chris says he is praying for one more miracle in his life—finding a sponsor who will help finance his efforts to go for the gold.

"When sponsors hear that I got shot they turn their backs on me, thinking that I'm a bad person. I'm not about that. I'm a senior at Ohio State University getting ready to graduate. I will make the 1996 Olympics, but right now I need a lot of assistance to help me pursue that dream."

Chris adds that when he does turn pro, he plans to use part of his earnings to improve sports facilities in the poor Columbus neighborhood where he grew up.

"I want to fix up the running track and put in new basketball hoops and things like that. A lot of athletes make it big and forget where they grew up. I'm going to do everything I can to help the kids from my neighborhood. . . ."

Man Narrowly Escapes Death—Three Times!

From Vietnam battlefields to the more peaceful confines of Washington, D.C., Fred Laughlin seems to be living a charmed life.

Three times the Price Waterhouse executive has faced almost certain death: once from a land mine during the war, and on two other occasions when disaster struck much closer to home. Each time he miraculously managed to survive his injuries.

Fred has little doubt that someone up there is watching over him, but these days it is not always the dramatic miracles—such as those that may have saved his life—upon which he dwells.

Instead, he likes to point to the smaller miracles that prove God's everyday presence in people's lives. He says all one has to do is look at the birds and the trees to understand exactly what he means....

It was 1967, and the war in Vietnam was still raging. Fred Laughlin, then a young infantry lieutenant, was on routine patrol with his outfit outside the small village of Lai

Khe, located between Saigon and Cambodia. The tall, red-haired soldier was prepared for danger, but not for an incident that nearly cost him his life.

Fred was riding on top of a "track," a personnel carrier used to transport infantrymen. Soldiers did not sit inside the vehicle in case it struck a land mine. The odds of survival by riding on top of the track were higher.

Around noon, disaster struck—the "track" ran over a 500-ton mine. The force of the huge explosion lifted the vehicle several feet off the ground, flipping it completely upside down as it fell back to the ground.

The 51-year-old veteran's voice takes on a grim tone as he relates what happened then. "There were several of us on that track; the impact of the explosion caused us to go flying through the air. The miracle is not just that I survived, but that everyone survived except the driver."

Fred was knocked unconscious. While he was unconscious, Fred remembers being in what he describes as a "dream sequence." He still finds it a bit difficult to explain exactly how he felt, and likens it to a television with the sound on, but no picture. "I could hear people all around me talking. I could hear what was going on but, as in a dream, I was observing but not really there."

Fred adds that his state of mind during those moments helps him appreciate "people who talk about having out-of-body experiences."

He regained full consciousness while being loaded into a rescue helicopter. His next memories are of lying in a hospital bed where he was treated for a severe leg wound and other injuries. As he lay there, Fred realized how miraculous it was that he and his other men had survived.

When he was finally discharged from the Army, Fred thought that there would be no more close brushes with death. He couldn't have been more wrong. Twice more he would narrowly escape being killed.

The Price Waterhouse partner, who today lives with his wife and family in Potomac, Maryland, had just joined his firm's Office of Government Services in Washington, D.C., when he had his second brush with death.

"I was commuting to work daily on my motorcycle. One day I was in the left-hand lane doing about 35 miles per hour and a car was coming from the other way," he recalls. "The other driver suddenly turned directly into my lane and hit me."

For the second time in less than 10 years, Fred found himself flying helplessly through the air, in an accident that could easily have proved fatal. His motorcycle was a mass of twisted metal, and blood streamed down his face.

Again, his luck held. Incredibly, no other cars on the highway ran over him as he lay on the asphalt. Despite deep cuts and lacerations, Fred's only major injury was to his leg—the same leg he had hurt in the mine incident in Vietnam. Again, Fred found himself in a hospital, this time for six weeks.

Several years later, Fred experienced his third narrow escape from death, this time while watching his son play in a Washington, D.C., lacrosse championship in 1991.

Fred had arrived at the game late, and saw ominous clouds gathering in the distance as the game progressed. When it began to rain, Fred joined others searching for cover. And then his luck nearly ran out.

"I opened my umbrella and lightning hit the tree I was standing under. The lightning came down the tree, struck my umbrella, and went down my arm." Lightning also struck and killed a student standing just a few feet away. Fred was knocked to the ground unconscious, and people who ran to his aid thought he was dead.

He was later told that his heart had stopped beating for several minutes. Again, Fred credits divine intervention for saving his life. Standing not far from him was a fire department volunteer proficient in lifesaving techniques.

"He started working on me. He gave me CPR and mouth-to-mouth resuscitation." Fred regained consciousness, and an ambulance parked on the grounds rushed him to the hospital in critical condition. Fred calls it "pretty miraculous" that both a volunteer fireman and an ambulance were nearby.

When word of what happened reached his wife and neighbors, an around-the-clock prayer vigil was organized for him as doctors struggled to save his life. Fred says he is convinced those prayers played a vital role in his recovery, and believes that God listens to prayers.

"If God didn't have the power to save people like myself, He wouldn't be God," he quietly philosophizes. "But why He chose to save me three times, I don't know."

While quietly counting his blessings, Fred likes to talk about the everyday presence of God in people's lives, not just dramatic moments. He urges people to open their eyes to the small everyday miracles all around them. "I guess that's what's really miraculous—His intervention in our everyday lives."

Wife Saves Husband's Life After Doctors Give Up

When astrologer and kinesiologist Joy Lisker walked into a hospital emergency room in Southern California and correctly diagnosed her husband's condition after doctors could not figure out what was wrong with him, that was only the beginning.

Later, when told that her husband had little chance of recovery, Joy, again, took matters into her own hands. She joined forces with a healer to save her husband's life.

Joy Lisker says she knew something was terribly wrong that September morning in 1989 when her husband, Robert, a 63-year-old attorney, woke up with a 103-degree fever.

"He was in bad shape, but it was a Sunday and the doctor I called wanted me to wait until Monday," she recalls. "I tried to keep Robert comfortable during the day, but by that evening I realized that he had to go to the hospital."

Joy drove Robert to the Sherman Oaks Hospital emergency room where "they started doing every kind of test imaginable, from X-rays to ultrasound," she says. The results of the tests puzzled the doctors, who were unable to pinpoint the cause of Robert's distress.

Joy approached her husband, who was awaiting treatment. "I told him, 'I'm going to find out what's wrong.'"

She began to apply her knowledge of kinesiology, a method of testing muscles to determine what is going on in the body. Before long, Joy realized that her husband had some kind of gallbladder infection—something doctors had already ruled out.

"I knew it wasn't gallstones, but an infection," she says. "I went over to his personal doctor and told him that it looked like a gallbladder problem. He looked at me and said, 'But Joy, there are no gallstones. If there are no gallstones, there's usually no problem.'"

Joy insisted that doctors perform additional tests. "They called me the first thing the very next morning," she says. Her diagnosis had been correct. "They said the situation was much more serious than they had anticipated, and they were preparing to operate immediately."

Doctors later told Joy that her diagnosis had saved her husband's life. "They said the gallbladder was ready to burst, and that would have been curtains for him."

The surgery was successful, but there was bad news still to come. Several days later, complications set in. "The doctor called me to say that everything had shut down, and Robert was in terrible shape. They were calling to prepare me for the worst."

Joy recalls that it was one of the darkest moments in her life. "I moped around the hospital, crying, not sure which way to go." By mid-afternoon she had made a decision. Joy picked up the phone and called a longtime friend, Dr. Judith Sakurai, a California chiropractor skilled in the use of crystals and other alternative-healing techniques.

"Judith arrived that evening. We went into Robert's room. First we used kinesiology on him to 'ask his body' if it wanted to be here. We wouldn't go against his wishes if he wanted to go." Robert indicated he wished to be helped. "Then, we asked his body through kinesiology whether this situation can be reversed," Joy says, "and we got a positive answer." Amazingly, Joy said it took Judith "no more than 15 or 20 minutes to do her thing."

The very next morning, Joy's phone rang. It was Robert's doctor with good news. "He said, 'Joy, everything has turned around.'" Excitedly, she hung up the phone. Her husband would live, after all.

Joy says it wasn't only her and Judith's efforts that were responsible for her husband's recovery. She also credits a daring doctor for his help.

"Robert's kidneys were no longer functioning, and his doctor came in and did the last thing you would think of," Joy says. "He felt he had nothing to lose and decided that this treatment was either going to kill him or cure him." The physician flooded Robert's kidneys with water. The gamble paid off.

"Now everything had turned around for the better. All his systems were working again." Meanwhile, Joy says that Judith continued to work with Robert, visiting him twice a day for the next three days.

"It was all pretty extraordinary," she says, looking back at those moments. "The doctors never thought he would walk out of there, and here he is today, perfectly healthy."

Saved by Angels

Some people can't seem to keep themselves out of hot water. Max Sobel, an 87-year-old retired New York City bartender, however, has always been much more affected by cold water in his life.

Twice in his younger days, Max nearly drowned in boating and swimming accidents. He was saved both times, he insists, by the miraculous appearance of guardian angels....

Max Sobel remembers being a reckless 19-year-old youth, horsing around in a canoe in New York City's Prospect Park.

"My friend told me to sit down, but since when does a teenager listen to any sound advice?" he asks. "We were halfway across the lagoon when the canoe turned upside down." Panic set in. Max could not swim.

"I was splashing around frantically; my friend had swum to a small island in the middle of the lagoon and was out of my sight. Suddenly, someone was swimming right next to me." As soon as the mysterious stranger appeared beside him, Max remembers feeling "as if I knew how to swim—

like I was swimming—but I didn't know how. It really was miraculous."

"He helped me make it back to shore, but when I went to thank him, nobody was there."

A year later, Max was back in the water, this time up to his waist in the ocean at Coney Island. "I was practicing swimming in the shallow water. Suddenly a huge wave came along and caught me by surprise. I tried to swim, but I just couldn't catch my breath—I was drowning."

What happened next astonishes him to this day.

"There was a man standing next to me. He must have been 10 feet tall, maybe even taller—I'm not exaggerating! He pulled me back to the shore."

Moments later, lifeguards appeared and gave Max artificial respiration. When Max asked them about the man who had saved him, the lifeguards exchanged looks. "We saw you swimming and struggling," they said. "There was nobody with you." Max maintains another angel rescued him.

"I'm convinced that it was an angel," he says. "This was a huge person. No human is 10 feet tall. I told everyone I knew about it." Max didn't care whether people believed him or not. "Maybe that's why I was rescued by angels.

Because I believe in them."

Max says his entire life has been blessed by guardian angels who have saved him from harm on several other occasions. None of the episodes, however, were as dramatic as the water rescues.

After the second mishap, and despite his belief that a guardian angel continues to watch over him, Max says he never again stepped foot in bodies of water.

"The closest I've been to water since Coney Island is in my shower!"

Child Conquers Cancer Against All Odds

This is a story about Michael, a very special child who, at three months of age, was diagnosed with a deadly form of cancer and given only a remote chance of survival.

Today, against all odds, Michael is an active and intelligent 16-year-old who, with wit and a sense of humor, is still courageously fighting an ongoing battle with that dread disease.

For Michael's mother, Linda Gillick, her son's story is one of hope. She says it should inspire and give courage to parents who may feel their world is ending when their child is diagnosed with cancer....

"I think Michael's a living miracle, because he's still going and he shouldn't be," says Linda Gillick, a resident of Toms River, New Jersey. "It's only by the grace of God that he's still going."

There's heartbreak in her voice, but also fierce pride in Michael's battle for life. After a moment of reflection, the mother of two, now a political activist for children stricken with cancer, continues:

"He's here for a purpose. I think he's opening the eyes of the world to appreciate life."

Linda also believes that Michael symbolizes what can happen to children and adults when the environment is destroyed by pollution.

She is firmly convinced that chemical pollution in her hometown is responsible for Michael's condition, and notes that chemical pollution is a leading contributor to rising cancer incidents among children throughout the nation.

"I consider Michael and all our children endangered species if this kind of pollution continues. Michael is a symbol to make people realize what can happen."

Michael's story begins in 1979. Linda, her husband, Rusty, and first son, Kevin, were an average family with everyday problems. When Mike was born, Linda says, "he was the most beautiful, perfect baby you have ever seen."

Three and one-half months later, when Michael began to spit up—something he had never done before—Linda says she didn't make too much of it.

"One day, we put him down for a nap, and when we went to pick him up about an hour later, his eyes were going back and forth in his head like a robot." Linda and Rusty rushed their baby to the doctor.

The doctor advised the Gillicks to have Michael examined by a neurologist. Little Michael's terrible ordeal had begun.

"The neurologist was so concerned that she called us on a Sunday morning, and we were in her office on Monday morning," Linda recalls. More tests were recommended, but nothing out of the ordinary was detected. So Michael was sent home with advice to the Gillicks to keep a close eye on their child. They did, and other unusual symptoms soon developed.

"When Michael was sleeping, he would begin to turn in his bed and scratch the mattress," Linda says. "When he would get into the car, he would throw up."

One day, while giving Michael his bath, Rusty discovered a lump on his son's body. "We rushed Michael to the doctor, again."

It was quickly discovered that Michael's kidney was pushing out of his back. This time the child was hospitalized. He was three and one-half months old.

Michael was eventually diagnosed with a rare and deadly form of cancer called neuroblastoma. To his doctors' amazement, tumors would actually begin to grow on the child's body as they watched. At one point, doctors told

Linda: "Your baby is in critical condition. We don't know if he'll make it through the night."

She remembers looking at the doctors as if they were crazy. "Here's this baby with big, blue, sparkling eyes, cooing away, smiling, and they're trying to tell me that he wouldn't live through the night."

An emergency operation followed. "The doctors took him in, opened him up, then closed him up again. Michael was given a 50/50 chance of survival."

For Linda and Rusty, the news was devastating. "I just kept thinking, this is a nightmare. This is not happening to this perfect, beautiful baby. When they told us it was cancer, I broke down. I became hysterical and started crying."

Linda says that by the end of July, Michael's doctors told her that he was not going to live.

"We had the choice of trying experimental drugs that had only been used on animals—he would remain in the hospital. Or we could take him home and try to keep him comfortable." After considering their choices, the Gillicks decided to take their son home.

It's been a long, difficult road ever since for Linda Gillick and her family. To this day, she has no idea where that road is leading. What she does know is that despite "many bad days," Michael is still dealing with his condition with a positive mental attitude and a great sense of humor.

"This kid is still smiling. He drives the doctors nuts," Linda says laughingly. "He still has the most charming, witty, amazing way about him. He can capture just about anybody's heart."

Which is why, she says, it is not really too surprising that over the years Michael has captured the hearts of celebrities such as actors Michael J. Fox and the late Michael Landon. Other celebrities and athletes—especially football players from the New York Giants—have also become some of Michael's biggest supporters.

"There's an extreme specialness about Michael," Linda says. "He's the story of a miracle. . . ."

Lost Daughter Finds Her Family

Given up for adoption at an early age, Glenda Jones says she never once lost hope of someday locating her biological parents, as well as the rest of her missing family.

Without any financial resources and motivated by a mysterious voice that whispered encouragement to her late at night, the 20-year-old nurse's assistant began a remarkable search to find her family.

Today, Glenda says she hopes that the story of her success will inspire others who are also searching for their birth parents. All it takes, she says, is hope, persistence, and the knowledge that if you want something badly enough, miracles can happen. . . .

Glenda Jones, 33, says she has read some detective novels over the years. She never dreamed, however, that someday she would be doing the kind of investigating that would eventually reunite her with a family she had not seen since she was four years old.

Glenda had no idea what had happened to her biological parents or her four brothers and sisters. The only clues she had to go on, she says, were childhood memories of friends and relatives. But Glenda believed that if she could still recognize those faces today, they would have some information about the whereabouts of her missing family.

There was also someone else helping with the search—a constant nighttime companion who she can only describe as her guardian angel. It was a voice in the night that kept urging her, "Don't give up, don't give up."

Glenda never did. Wherever she went, her eyes would scan faces all around her to see if anyone looked familiar. If anyone did, Glenda put aside her shyness and began asking them questions.

"I was like a detective. I would say to them, 'Do you know my mother?' Some of these people I hadn't seen since I was 11 years old, but they still looked familiar to me."

One day, a hunch worked out for her. Glenda was in a Columbus, Georgia, church at the time, and thought one of the worshipers looked like a boy she knew as a child.

"I walked up to him and said, 'Hey, do you know me?' He said, 'No.' But I said, 'I'm sure I know you.' I started to pressure this guy to remember me."

The young man stared blankly at her. He had no memory of her whatsoever. Glenda still believed that she once knew him. "I went home and said, 'I know I'm not wrong. God knows I'm not wrong.' So I went back to that church and I saw him again—it was two months later—and I reminded him of things that happened when he was six years old and we were in church together."

Still, she could not jog the young man's memory. So Glenda tried a different tack. She asked whether his mother was still alive, and whether she would agree to speak to Glenda. "It turned out that his mother was one of my mother's cousins, and she had an idea where my mother was living," Glenda says.

Glenda was breathless. She believed that this lead to her mother's whereabouts was nothing short of a miracle. "It's even more miraculous that, even though I was adopted at four, I never really forgot anybody and remembered faces.

"In 1978, I finally traced my biological mother. She was living in Birmingham, Alabama, at the time." After a tearful reunion, Glenda's mother helped her search for the rest of her missing family. "Through her, I began to find my other brothers and sisters, even though she had no real idea where they were living."

One year later, Glenda located her biological father by tracing him through his parents. "I met my father in 1979 when I graduated from high school," she says. "He was living in New York City." Glenda flew East for the emotional reunion. But her efforts didn't end there.

There was still one missing brother she had failed to locate. Glenda was determined to find him as well. "No one had seen him or knew where he might be," she recalls. After hours on the telephone, her persistence paid off. She found her missing brother living in Mississippi. He was 17 years old at the time.

Within eight years after her search began, Glenda had single-handedly managed to locate her biological parents, all four of her brothers and sisters, and both of her grandmothers. The task seems even more incredible, since her family was scattered throughout the United States.

Reflecting upon her success, Glenda says, "It is one of the greatest miracles of my life to be adopted and still see all of my family. I continue to stay in touch with all of them."

Finding her biological family changed her life, Glenda says. Before then, she always felt a bit depressed, as if a piece of her was missing.

"Even though I was adopted and taken care of, I wanted to know everything about my past. Now I do. That, to me, is the most miraculous thing in the world. Some people are adopted and they're lost. They don't really know who they are. That's how I felt. The minute I found my parents it helped turn my life around."

Glenda encourages other adopted children seeking their kin never to quit their search. "I was smart enough to find people who were lost to me without spending money," she says. "I used my own time, and I did all this on my own. Anyone who believes in miracles can do the same."

The Legendary White Buffalo... Reborn?

Among the Plains Indians, a legend still recounted in the sweat lodges and around ceremonial campfires tells of a mysterious woman who appeared to the tribes long ago. She brought with her a sacred pipe that allowed the tribal members to speak to the spirits.

One night while she was with the Lakota Sioux, the woman turned to leave. As the tribespeople watched her go, a marvelous thing happened. The woman turned into a white buffalo!

According to the legend, when the white buffalo returns, she will bring with her a period of peace and prosperity.

Has the woman-turned-white buffalo's spirit returned today to a farm in southern Wisconsin, where a rare white buffalo calf was born in 1994? Is this rare and mythical buffalo, indeed, a Native American miracle...?

Janesville, Wisconsin, is a small town about 100 miles northeast of Chicago. Just outside this town of 55,000 people, Dave and Valerie Heider operate a farm that has always been a curiosity to their neighbors—even before the birth of the crowd-drawing rare white buffalo, aptly named "Miracle" by its owners.

While most farmers in that corner of the state raise cows and produce Wisconsin's world-renowned cheeses, the Heiders have always been a bit more adventurous about their choice of farm animals.

So when the couple decided in 1989 to breed buffalo as part of their exotic animal collection—which already included peacocks and a llama—neighbors shook their heads and went about their business.

But even Dave Heider, usually unflappable when it comes to his farm animals, was in for a shock the morning of August 20, 1994. Among his herd of 13 brown, shaggy-haired North American bison, was a ghostly white calf.

"You can't print what I said," he says. "This was awesome!"

Dave excitedly picked up his phone and called a friend who writes for agricultural publications. Soon, word of the occurrence began to spread. The Heiders' phone started ringing nonstop, and cars began showing up at the farm.

"I'll tell you one thing," he quips, "If another one is born, I'm not telling anybody!"

Once Dave learned of the white buffalo's significance, he decided to open up his farm and let people see the animal, rather than sell it to those clamoring to buy it—including rock musician Ted Nugent.

"How can you put a price tag on something unique?" he asks. "How are you going to put a price tag on a sacred belief? Besides, this calf has brought people together from around the world, and that's good."

Interest in the beautiful white buffalo has not lessened. Each week, Miracle continues to attract hundreds of people to the Heider farm, especially Native Americans, who believe they are witnessing a legend come to life.

The Heiders often hear their Native American visitors praise them for not selling the animal to those who may have exploited her.

"They don't look at Miracle as a rare bison, but as a vision," Heider says. "Their spiritual connection to the buffalo is awesome."

For Etta Little Thunder, a 78-year-old Lakota Sioux from South Dakota, the birth of the white buffalo is a Native American miracle. She describes the animal as "very symbolic of our culture, reminding us of a more spiritual life."

Dave says Native Americans who visit his farm leave many tokens as offerings to Miracle. "There are feathers and fetishes, handwritten prayers, medicine wheels, and even pouches of herbs."

He also notes that Miracle is a magnet for many others who are not Native Americans—people who practice alternative and Native American ways of life. "They set up sweat lodges, beat drums, shake sticks, and conduct various rituals in the area," he says with a touch of amusement.

Is the birth of the white buffalo truly a Native American miracle? Has the woman-turned-white buffalo's spirit returned after all these years?

"No matter what your point of view, the fact remains that this is a rare birth," says Floyd Hand, a Lakota Sioux spiritual healer. Hand led hundreds of Native Americans in a ceremony to commemorate the reappearance of the woman-turned-white buffalo's spirit after the calf was born. "White buffalo are so rare that there's no real consensus on just how rare they are. This birth may be a one-in-10-million occurrence. Does that make it a miracle? Why not?"

Near-Fatal Accident Brings a Glimpse of Paradise

Are near-death experiences a miracle of sorts, allowing those who undergo them a glimpse of what awaits all of us when we die? Or, as some scientists suggest, are they simply a psychological reaction to the idea of death?

All Elinor Gadon knows for certain is that her near-death experience felt quite real. For long moments when she was presumed dead after an automobile accident, she says she was very much alive—but in a different time and place. A place she calls Paradise. . . .

Elinor Gadon refrains from describing her near-death experience as a miracle. "The miracle," she says, "is that I didn't cut the main artery in my neck when that car broad-sided my Volkswagen and my head went through the windshield."

What followed this accident was an experience that left her convinced that death is not the final moment. "There's something that comes after when what we know as life ends," Elinor says. "I don't know if that something is forever—I haven't any idea whether there's reincarnation—but at least for a time there is life after death."

The accident took place in Peabody, Massachusetts. Elinor was then a young mother and graduate student driving three of her children, aged 10, 12 and 14, to a shopping mall. The trip was in preparation for the family's planned move to India, where her husband, Herman, had just accepted a job.

Tragedy struck in the form of another car, whose driver was apparently blinded by the sun's glare. The large vehicle plowed into Elinor's Volkswagen, and the impact of the crash smashed her head into the windshield, shattering the glass. The broken glass slashed her chin and jaw from ear to ear, and the steering-wheel column shattered her sternum. Half her body was left hanging out the window. Elinor appeared to be dead.

However, she was not experiencing pain or the fear of death at that moment, but what she describes as ecstasy! "I was hovering maybe 300 or 400 feet off the ground," she recalls. "I felt only peace—as if I was in Paradise. There was this marvelous garden and everything smelled so sweet. I felt so good, like nothing else I'd ever experienced."

While her spirit hovered above, Elinor could clearly observe what was going on at the accident site below. "I saw the policeman come, and the car—and then I realized that my children were crying. My body was hanging through the windshield and they thought I was dead."

Elinor was unable to ignore the heart-wrenching sound of her crying children. It drew her back to painful reality. "The birth of a child is the greatest miracle in life, and I think I willed myself to live because I knew that my children needed me."

She remembers how difficult it was to "let go of Paradise" and return to her physical body, but Elinor says she willed herself to do exactly that. "What I actually did was force myself to become conscious, then I pulled my body out of the windshield," she says.

Once back in her body, the first thing she recalls doing is reassuring her children that their father would soon arrive to take care of them. "My face was cut, and I realized that I was bleeding. I told the policeman to take me to the best hospital in the area."

At the hospital, doctors stitched up her chin and jaw. The young woman had nearly bled to death because of her injuries.

Six weeks later, Elinor and her family were off to India. While she never forgot the incident, Elinor didn't speak of her experience for years afterward, fearing ridicule. It was only after a friend told her about the work of Elisabeth Kubler-Ross, a leading researcher in the field of life after death, that Elinor discovered her experience was not unusual.

"When I heard about what she had to say, it gave me shivers," Elinor says. "I realized that this was a phenomenon that lots of people had experienced—not just me."

The accident changed the tone and direction of Elinor's life. Since the accident, she has gone on to get a doctorate degree in the history of culture at the University of Chicago and to teach art history, comparative religion, and Indian culture at Harvard and Tufts universities. Today, she is also developing a women's spirituality program at the California Institute for Integral Studies in San Francisco, where she lives.

"It was a very real experience for me. It gave me permission to believe in something larger than what I knew. There's a true mystery here."

Recipe for a Miracle Cure

Pam Dungy never expected to survive after she was diagnosed with a bone tumor near the brain. Nor did she anticipate the outpouring of prayer from her students, friends, and others who learned of her illness.

But most of all, the 47-year-old California teacher never expected to find herself baking a huge gingerbread house—a holiday gift for her doctor and his staff—two weeks before her scheduled surgery.

There's one more thing that Pam never expected: that a miracle would occur just moments before her surgery was scheduled to begin....

When she began experiencing dizziness and other medical problems two years ago, Pam Dungy decided to pay a visit to her family doctor. After examining Pam, her doctor suggested that she schedule an appointment with a neurologist for some testing. When the tests were completed, Pam learned the bad news. A tumor had appeared in a bone located close to her brain.

Pam, who teaches English as a second language to refugees in Fresno, California, was referred to the

University of California, San Francisco Medical Center. Doctors there told her that surgery would be required.

Pam was given the name of Dr. Charles Wilson, chief of the hospital's neurological unit, as the top specialist in this field. She was also told that his caseload was so heavy, he might not be able to take her on as a patient.

"Getting to see Dr. Wilson is a long process," she says. "Everyone wants to see him because he's the best." Pam lucked out. She was accepted as a patient as a result of a phone call from her doctor's daughter—also a physician—who convinced the specialist to see Pam.

"He looked at my medical workups and agreed that the problem definitely needed to be addressed. He asked to see me on December 8, just before the holiday season." Pam was pleased, but terribly upset.

"I was real scared at that time about whether the tumor had penetrated the brain or was about to. If that happened, there wasn't a lot they could do."

She was assured that nothing of the sort had happened, but that surgery still would be required. "I thought about my three young kids and wondered if I would see them in the spring," Pam says. Meanwhile, as word of her condition spread, Pam's family and friends began to hold prayer vigils.

One evening Pam received a phone call from a close friend, a priest on a religious retreat in Vancouver, Canada. "He had found out about my tumor from his order and called that night. He said that he'd been praying for me since 10 o'clock that morning."

It struck Pam as odd that, although she'd had no idea of the priest's prayers for her, all that day she felt "as if this peace was taking over me."

That feeling seemed to increase when she learned how many people were praying for her. "Once the prayers began, my fear subsided. I felt peaceful. I didn't expect the tumor to be gone, but I knew that, whether I lived or died, I could handle it, that it would be okay."

When Pam arrived for her appointment with Dr. Wilson, the reception room was filled with patients waiting to see him. The specialist frequently came into the waiting area to cheer up his patients. "It was extraordinary to see how much hope he gave them. It was miraculous both that I could get in to see him in such a short time, and to see his relationship with his patients."

Once seated in Dr. Wilson's office, Pam says she could hardly restrain expressing her admiration for the specialist. "I kept thinking that God has given him an extraordinary gift to help people. There was a feeling that God was working through him. I was just so impressed."

When she left Dr. Wilson's office that day, Pam decided that she had to give the physician and his staff a special gift. "On the way back from the hospital I told my husband that I really have to do something for this remarkable doctor."

With the surgery only two weeks away, Pam found herself in her kitchen the next morning baking a gingerbread house. "I went home and spent three days making this elaborate gingerbread house with all the symbols of Christmas on it. I put a lot of spirit into it."

Even today she is amazed at that time in her life. "It's extraordinary when I look back and think. How could I have done all that during this period of time? I was going in for major surgery in two weeks."

Pam showed up at the hospital a day before her surgery carrying the gingerbread house. Everyone at the hospital was delighted with her thoughtfulness. The next morning, she returned to the hospital for her scheduled surgery.

As the time for her operation neared, Pam was approached by a nurse who told her that Dr. Wilson had ordered an additional MRI exam, an in-depth type of X-ray.

"I wondered why they were doing that now. I was kind of psyched up to get the surgery over with."

When the nurse returned with the test results, she had an inquisitive look on her face. "She asked, 'What are you here for?' I told her I was here to be treated for a tumor."

The nurse patted Pam's knee and said, "I think we may have some good news for you today."

"I remember thinking that maybe this thing was gone," Pam recalls, "but I didn't say anything to my husband."

Another MRI was taken. This time the nurse had nothing to say. Nonetheless, Pam says she had a good feeling. "This time I said to my husband, 'Maybe the tumor's gone.'" She remembers the incredulous look on her husband's face. After all, the tumor was the size of a golf ball and it wasn't likely it could suddenly disappear.

Thirty minutes later, Pam's name was called. She was told by a nurse to report to Dr. Wilson's office. "They whisked us in and he said, 'First of all, I want to wish you a very merry Christmas. Secondly, your tumor is gone and you can go home.'"

Pam felt as if she were in a dream. "I hugged him and I kissed him. Then I went over to my husband and did the same. I was just speechless."

She finally gathered her composure and asked the specialist what had happened. Dr. Wilson simply shrugged his shoulders.

"He said he just didn't know, and that they would have to do a lot of looking at everything. He said, 'All I know is that the tumor is completely gone. I couldn't have done a better job if I had gone in there with a scalpel.'"

As Pam was about to leave Dr. Wilson's office, he had some final words for her. "I'm available for you any time in the future. Just don't take back your gingerbread house!" They all laughed.

Pam has returned to the hospital for tests several times since. The results have always been the same: no tumor. "What happened to me was nothing less than a miracle."

Surprise Check Arrives in Answer to a Prayer

Dr. Eileen Nauman, a homeopathic practitioner and Native American shaman, has always placed strong faith in her spiritual beliefs. So, in time of financial need, it was not unusual for her to turn to the Great Spirit of her Cherokee roots for help.

When Eileen required an expensive computer program to help her ailing clients, but could not afford the price, the brown-haired, blue-eyed healer says all it took was a softly spoken Native American prayer and a simple ritual, for a miracle to occur. The money for the software arrived in the next day's mail....

When Eileen Nauman, who lives just outside Sedona, Arizona, received a brochure about a new software system, she decided the program was essential to her growing homeopathic medical practice. It provided important diagnostic information, along with vital data about vitamins and minerals quickly and concisely. It would not only speed her ability to handle her current patients' needs, but would allow her to help more people as well.

The $999.99 price, however, was more than Eileen could afford to spend at the time.

"They were only having a special on it for a certain number of days," she recalls, "and I got the mailer late. This was the last day to call and say, 'Yes, I want it.'"

She called, anyway, asking whether the company would allow her to pay in installments. They refused.

"In addition to my homeopathic practice, I write books for a living," she says. "I get paid twice a year in royalties, in May and November, but I never know what the amount is going to be. This happened in April, so there was the possibility of money coming in next month, but I had no way of knowing for sure."

Because of that uncertainty, Eileen's husband, David, was reluctant to charge the purchase on their credit card. Because money was tight, he worried that they would not be able to make the payments.

But there was no doubt in Eileen's mind that she needed the system in order to better serve her patients. "So I made a command decision to buy the software. I told Dave that I had a good feeling about it, and that I was going to go for it." This is when Eileen turned to the Great Spirit of her Native American religion.

"I have Cherokee blood, so I said a prayer to the Great Spirit. I said, 'I hope you can support my decision on this.' I talk quite often to the Great Spirit because of work I also do as a shaman."

A shaman, she explains, is a healer in touch with ancient spirits. She adds that virtually every religion and philosophy throughout the world has their shamans, and Native Americans are no exception.

"I have a good pipeline to the Great Spirit," Eileen adds, "and he/she knows that I'm of good moral quality and integrity, and I would only ask for things like this software if it were going to help a lot of other people. So I said, 'Thy will be done,' and I let the prayer go."

After she concluded the simple ritual, Eileen again brought up the matter with her husband, Dave. "I repeated that I felt we would be supported in this. It was a hunch or an instinct."

Dave agreed, so the couple charged the purchase on their credit card. They hoped that money would arrive from somewhere to pay the bill when it arrived.

The next day, Eileen's husband returned from work with a broad grin on his face. "I asked, 'What are you smiling about?' and he handed me an envelope."

She opened the envelope, and was stunned to find a royalty check for $1,000—one cent more than the price of the software system!

"This was really out of the blue, neither of us knew that this one was coming." Eileen adds that so infrequent are payments from this project, "that we sometimes even forget about it. It's such an up-and-down thing, we don't even add it into our budget."

Eileen sees a direct connection between her prayers to the Great Spirit and the arrival of the $1,000 check. "To me, that was a real miracle because we were really sweating it. We'd been living hand-to-mouth, and now we could afford to pay for the software...."

The Miracle of True Love

Eleanor and Harry had nearly given up hope of ever finding their soulmates. Both had spent long years in a fruitless search for true love.

But just when things seemed darkest, Eleanor and Harry met in a most unusual way. While some friends chalk it up to coincidence, Eleanor views things quite differently. She says meeting Harry was nothing less than a miracle of love....

Eleanor Soohoo, 41, an administrative assistant for a hotel management company, has always described herself as a bit of a rebel.

Unlike many members of her family, the Armenian-born woman says she did not want to take part in an arranged marriage. Instead, she dreamed of something much less practical and far more romantic: finding her Prince Charming in the United States.

"Armenians are very family-connected and traditional people," she explains. "But as a young girl growing up there, I always dreamed about coming to America and having this fairy-tale life."

The attractive, New Canaan, Connecticut, woman believed she was on the way to realizing her dream when her family decided to emigrate to the United States. But after arriving in New York City in 1974, disappointment quickly set in. Finding love would have to take second place to financial survival.

"Here I was in this new country thinking that I was going to meet Prince Charming, but I spent more time trying to find a job, helping my family who couldn't speak English, and just surviving," she says.

Time passed swiftly with no prospect for a husband in sight. Although Eleanor met and dated several young men—each time hoping this would be the husband she so longed for—the relationships failed.

There's a trace of sadness in her voice as she recalls: "They weren't my Prince Charming. I was meeting people, but I wasn't getting close to them. I was getting more and more disappointed."

Even more discouraging, Eleanor watched brothers, sisters, cousins, and other relatives get married, while she remained single. As the only one in the family still without a husband, more and more family responsibilities fell on her shoulders.

She giggles as she recollects how desperate she had become in her fruitless search for a husband. "I tried to date everyone. I went through a lot of stupid phases. It just never worked. I was always disappointed, and I felt crushed."

Finally, at age 38, Eleanor decided she had had enough. She would simply abandon her search for true love. Her Prince Charming, she thought, must be living somewhere else. Perhaps she was just one of those women destined never to be married.

Eleanor called her girlfriend and said, "I'm not going to date anymore. I'm going to stay single." For a while, she even considered entering a convent.

Then, fate stepped in. Eleanor's friend happened across a newspaper ad for "Conscious Singles," a New Age singles group that was just forming and soliciting new members.

Her girlfriend pressed her to join the club, but Eleanor was not interested. "I didn't even want to try it, because I had been hurt so many times. I thought at the time that life was really a bad thing."

Finally, she agreed to sign up "just for fun." When Eleanor examined the club's list of eligible bachelors, her eyes went directly to one named Harry. "Harry was the first person I called," she says with amusement. "His ad seemed so modest."

Little did she then realize that Harry, a computer analyst, would eventually become her husband. Nor did Eleanor know at the time that, like her own family, Harry's Cantonese family had also emigrated to the United States. She learned after speaking to him on the phone that he, too, had spent long years in a fruitless search for a loving relationship.

"As a matter of fact, he had even more heartbreaking stories than I did, including a marriage that did not work. We shared the same dream of someday meeting somebody as if in a fairy tale."

Harry had also reluctantly decided to join the singles' club—at almost exactly the same time that she had—and also only because friends encouraged him to do so. It was if fate had arranged their meeting, she says.

So uncanny were the similarities in their backgrounds, Eleanor says that "listening to Harry talk about his life was almost like listening to myself speak. We both were at the stage where we didn't want to date anybody."

Eleanor held her breath. Was this the man for whom she had been searching for so long? "From the first moment, I had a sense that, this time, things might turn out differently. We were on the phone for two hours, and he told me he had to see me."

Still, Eleanor delayed meeting Harry in person, fearful of again being disappointed in love. It was now the beginning of the Christmas season, and Harry continued to call her. Finally, she agreed to meet him at a mall where she planned to do her holiday shopping.

"I drove to the mall and saw him for the first time. He was so cute standing there waiting for me." Eleanor remembers how Harry couldn't "take his eyes off me the whole time I was shopping. I finally said, 'Would you stop staring at me.' He said, 'I can't, you're so beautiful.'"

Eleanor describes what happened next as a Christmas miracle. Her voice still reflects some of the joy of that moment. "He said he wanted to spend the rest of his life with me. I couldn't believe it." Harry proposed to her a month later on New Year's Eve. Eleanor eagerly accepted. She knew her dream had finally come true.

"He was crying like a baby," she recalls with a giggle in her voice. "I just never felt with anyone else how I felt with him. I'd been taking care of my father, who was ill, and had been giving, giving, giving. I never thought I would find someone who would love me and who would want to give to me."

Eleanor insists that finding Harry was a miracle because "I prayed for it. I always talked to God. Just before I met Harry, I remember going into my room and pounding on the floor and saying, 'It's time, God, please let me meet someone. You know how much I've suffered. Let me find one good man who will love me and take care of me.'" Then Eleanor met Harry.

For people still looking for true love, Eleanor suggests that they, too, pray that it comes their way. "I wish everyone the same kind of miracle, and I know that if you pray for it hard enough to happen, it will happen. After all, I met Harry, didn't I?"

Priest Performs a Miraculous Healing

A paraplegic confined to a wheelchair for two decades, Leo Perras's thoughts often focused more on death than on life. Depressed about his condition, at times he felt almost eager to put an end to 20 years of pain and suffering.

What Leo hardly expected was a miracle that would change his life—one that came his way in the form of a priest renowned for his ability to heal.

Today, the man who never expected to walk again has resumed a normal, pain-free life... on his own two feet!

For 20 years, Easthampton, Massachusetts, resident Leo Perras, 73, had seen life from the grim perspective of a wheelchair.

Leo's medical problems began at 18, when he ruptured a disk lifting heavy equipment at the textile factory where he worked. He underwent a sacroiliac fusion, and spent seven months in a body cast.

Several months after the cast was removed, Leo was back in the hospital suffering from acute back pain. "The doctors stopped the pain, but I had a ruptured disc and nothing was done to treat it," he says. "This was back in the 1930s, when they didn't know much about ruptured discs."

Leo eventually returned to work, forced to wear a body cast and steel brace. Then, one morning he received a surprise notice from the draft board.

"Believe it or not, despite my medical history, they took me into the service," he says. "Six weeks later I went on a 10-mile hike with a full field pack and that did it."

Leo collapsed. He was rushed to the nearest Army hospital, where the doctors were amazed that he had been drafted in the first place. Leo was discharged from the Army two days later, at age 23.

When Leo returned home, he married and found work doing construction. He says that's when "all hell broke loose" with his body. Again, he was hospitalized. A second operation followed.

"Everything seemed to go well when I had a brace on. But the minute an orderly opened up the brace to give me a backrub, I felt as if I had been electrocuted."

Leo says he will never forget that moment's excruciating pain. "I arched backward and my head and heels tried to come together, I was in such agony."

Other operations followed. His life became a nightmare of pain, drugs to relieve the pain, and more surgery. Despite all this, Leo was still able to walk and to work.

When Leo began to fall for no apparent reason, he became depressed. After all, he now had a wife and children to support. If he couldn't stand, he couldn't work.

Back to the hospital he went, where yet another operation was performed, one that drastically altered his life.

"I woke up paralyzed from the rib cage down. That was it. For me, it was the end of the world. What was I going to do? I had five children at home."

A month later, Leo was released from the hospital in a wheelchair, unable to walk. He had become a paraplegic. More grief was in store for him. "A year later, I was in terrible pain, which happens in a lot of paraplegic cases," he says. "So I went back for surgery again."

But things only got worse. He emerged from surgery with a paralyzed left arm, along with other serious physical ailments. "My left eye was closed, I couldn't pass any water and I was still in pain," he says.

After a two-and-a-half month hospital stay, doctors told Leo's wife to take her husband home. Nothing more could be done for him.

For the next 10 months, Leo was mostly confined to his bed. Then, hoping his paralysis was not permanent, Leo began to consult with other specialists. They confirmed the worst—that he would never walk again. "I finally resigned myself to the fact that that was the way it would be," he says.

Although confined to a wheelchair, Leo tried to keep busy. He performed volunteer duties at a hospital, and sometimes worked light carpentry jobs. Because of his skills as a cabinetmaker, he even supervised part of a carpentry project at the hospital where he did volunteer work.

But more personal disaster awaited him. A year later, Leo was lying in a bed at that hospital with a case of bleeding ulcers so severe that he lapsed into a temporary coma.

Amazingly, Leo survived that ordeal, but his medical problems continued. In fact, they seemed to multiply. Leo underwent surgery in which half of his stomach was removed. Next, he was treated for a series of head and ear ailments, followed by treatment for a malfunctioning gallbladder, and, finally, arthritis.

"My doctor said, 'I don't know what to do with you anymore. Every week there's something new,'" Leo recalls.

When Leo's doctor suggested he go see Father Ralph DiOrio, a priest with a reputation for healing who would be lecturing in the area, Leo thought the physician was kidding. He wasn't.

"He even sent his wife to purchase tickets for me," Leo recalls. "When I found out about it, I said I wasn't going anywhere. I was in so much pain, I didn't want to go out of the house, period." Leo remained at home the evening of the lecture.

But that was not the last time that Leo was to hear about the faith healer. When his wife's former teacher, a nun, visited their home, Father DiOrio's name came up again. Leo learned that the priest was planning another appearance nearby.

Again, Leo was skeptical. But this time, under a great deal of pressure from his family, he reluctantly agreed to go.

It was a decision that would change his life.

"I went to the lecture with the intention of praying for my youngest daughter, who was having marital problems. When I got there, I couldn't believe what I saw. There were about 2,000 people outside the church."

The service began at 3 P.M. Leo recalls that there were more than two dozen other wheelchairs lined up next to his in front of the church's first pew.

"By 6 P.M., my pain was so bad, I turned to look at my wife, who was sitting behind me. She knew I was getting ready to leave," he says.

But a remark by the speaker delayed him from leaving. "Father DiOrio said that many healings had been performed that afternoon, but what he wanted was a healing that was visual, that people could relate to. I wanted to see what would happen."

Leo clearly remembers his surprise when the healer strode toward him.

"First, he blessed me with holy water. Then, he said a prayer and put his hand out, saying, 'In the name of Jesus Christ, rise.' "

Leo's voice cracks with emotion as he recalls this amazing moment.

"I didn't even realize that I was standing until I was face-to-face with him. Then I looked down at my legs and said, 'Oh my God.' "

Leo pauses as he struggles to control himself. With a deep breath, he continues: "Father DiOrio said, 'Bend down and touch your toes.' I had no muscles left. Everything was gone. Yet I bent down to touch my toes, and when I straightened up the pain was totally gone."

Father DiOrio asked Leo how long he had been confined to a wheelchair. "Twenty years," he replied. Father DiOrio said, "You and I are going to walk down the center aisle together to the front door of the church and back." Father DiOrio walked backward, praying, and Leo followed him.

Leo remembers with a chuckle the reaction that caused among his family and friends. "They were so startled to see me walk, they started to go bananas. One of my pals was standing on a pew hollering encouragement, and there's his wife reminding him that he's in church!"

Leo could not believe what was happening.

"I walked back to my wife, who said, 'How are you feeling?' I looked at her in disbelief and said 'The pain and the paralysis are gone.' She said, 'You must be tired, why don't you sit down?' I said, 'I've been sitting for 20 years!' I stood up for the rest of the service and left the church pushing my own chair."

Leo knocked on his doctor's door later that evening. "He was in shock. He asked me in and kept staring at me as he examined me. He said, 'You have no muscles, no reflexes, nothing to walk with. But I have to believe what I see.' And then he knelt down and started to pray."

Leo says he has not sat still since that miraculous day. He now devotes much of his time to traveling throughout the United States and Canada to give inspirational talks.

"I go out and pray with people. That's been my whole life since then. I want people to know not to give up hope, that miracles can always happen."